The
SWIMMER
of
AUSCHWITZ

The
SWIMMER
of
AUSCHWITZ

The Incredible True Story of the Olympic Hero Who Swam For His Life

RENAUD LEBLOND

monoray

First published in Great Britain in 2025 by Monoray,
an imprint of Octopus Publishing Group Ltd
Carmelite House
50 Victoria Embankment
London EC4Y 0DZ
www.octopusbooks.co.uk

An Hachette UK Company
www.hachette.co.uk

The authorized representative in the EEA is Hachette Ireland,
8 Castlecourt Centre, Dublin 15, D15 XTP3, Ireland (email: info@hbgi.ie)

Originally published by L'Archipel under the title *Le Nageur d'Auschwitz*
in 2022. This book is based on the true story of Alfred Nakache.

Copyright © L'Archipel, 2022
Translation copyright © Octopus Publishing Group Ltd, 2025

Distributed in the US by Hachette Book Group
1290 Avenue of the Americas, 4th and 5th Floors
New York, NY 10104

Distributed in Canada by Canadian Manda Group
664 Annette St., Toronto, Ontario, Canada M6S 2C8

All rights reserved. No part of this work may be reproduced or utilized
in any form or by any means, electronic or mechanical, including
photocopying, recording or by any information storage and retrieval
system, without the prior written permission of the publisher.

Renaud Leblond asserts the moral right to be
identified as the author of this work.

ISBN: 978-1-80096-296-5
eISBN: 978-1-80096-298-9

A CIP catalogue record for this book is available from the British Library.

Translation from French: Rae Walter in association with
First Edition Translations Ltd, Cambridge, UK

Picture acknowledgements: xiii Keystone-France/Gamma-Keystone
via Getty Images; 229 AFP via Getty Images

Typeset in 10.5/16pt Plantin MT Pro by
Six Red Marbles UK, Thetford, Norfolk

Printed and bound in Great Britain

1 3 5 7 9 10 8 6 4 2

This FSC® label means that materials used for the product
have been responsibly sourced.

This monoray book was crafted and published by Jake Lingwood, Mala
Sanghera-Warren, Alex Stetter, Rae Walter, Mel Four and Sarah Parry.

To Alice, Valentine, Nicolas and Pauline

'Once he has touched the water,
the swimmer is alone.'
Charles Sprawson, *Haunts of the Black Masseur:
The Swimmer as Hero*

'There would always be this memory, this solitude:
this snow in all the suns, this smoke in all the springs.'
Jorge Semprun, *Literature or Life*

Contents

CONTENTS

Alfred Nakache, 1938.

Constantine, Algeria, summer 1928

They won't force him into the water. Alfred doesn't like the water. He's told them so a thousand times. Every Saturday it's the same ritual, the same procession, the entire Nakache family hurrying down the sloping path that leads to the Sidi M'Cid swimming pool at the bottom of the Rhumel river gorge in Constantine, eastern Algeria.

'I keep telling you I don't like water, leave me alone!'

'Just say straight out that you're scared of it. You're such a wimp!' sneers his cousin Gilbert.

The worst of it is that he's right. Alfred is thirteen years old and the sea frightens him, as do ponds, even quite shallow ones. He doesn't know where this fear comes from. Sitting on the edge of the swimming pool, he clings to the little metal ladder going down into the blue water. He can barely manage to dip in his feet. Meanwhile, Prosper, his little brother, is swimming an increasing number of lengths, alternating between breaststroke and crawl, and making a point of pulling a different face at him every time he turns at this end of the pool.

Alfred pretends not to see him, looking up at the sun with his eyes half closed. His father, David, doesn't like the water either. What he likes is having all his family around him. Rose – Alfred's stepmother, who happens to be the sister of his mother who passed away too soon – his daughter Georgette, his sons, his nephews. Best of all he likes the moment when it's time for the picnic that has been carefully prepared by Sarah, the wonderful grandmother who, despite her dreadful short-sightedness and weak heart, excels herself in creatively satisfying the appetites of the entire tribe.

Every Saturday, the Sabbath, is a treat: little meat pies, aubergine caviar, dried tomatoes warmed by the sun and salted, houmous, orange salads, makroud biscuits filled with dates, pastries flavoured with rose water and orange flower water . . . They settle down in a shady corner overlooking the swimming pool where they are sheltered from the heat, close enough to enjoy watching the suntanned bodies of the divers as they hang in space but far enough from the hubbub to hear David telling his stories.

He never talks about his job managing a pawnshop. Alfred has barely taken in the fact that his father lends money to the city's most impoverished people. But when it comes to religion, Alfred's father can carry on talking forever. He's a true believer, and eager to teach all his offspring the principles of Judaism, the sacred texts, the Talmud, the Torah.

Alfred is a little ashamed to admit it, but he finds his father's long speeches a bit boring. He can't imagine what the God he talks about looks like, or where he's hiding. And mainly he can't imagine why, if God was up there watching over us, he wouldn't prevent all these awful things from happening. Here's one, by chance, on the front page of the local newspaper, *La Dépêche de Constantine*, which the rose hips are wrapped in: the attack of 22 January 1928, a bomb in the heart of the market – three people dead, two Jews and one Muslim, forty injured. Just people out doing their shopping, who happened to be passing by and hadn't done anything to anyone.

In the crumpled newspaper, he reads, without properly understanding, that it was another attack on the Jewish quarter, the Kar Chara as it was known, a disorderly maze of thousand-year-old alleyways on the far side of this city built on a rocky plateau, eight hundred metres above the Rhumel river. The neighbourhood ends at the Boulevard de l'Abîme – the boulevard of the abyss. *What was God doing that day?* Alfred doesn't ask his father. It would upset him too much. No, what Alfred likes to do down by the pool is talk about football with Roger, the youngest of the brothers. For two years they have been closely following the ups and downs of the Club Sportif Constantinois, the oldest team in Algeria, as if they were Real Madrid or Red Star, their favourite French football club.

Alfred's favourite player is Paul Nicolas, Red Star's striker. No one else in Saint-Ouen-sur-Seine can pierce the defence like him, it seems. Alfred admires his speed and power. Prosper likes Alex Thépot, the goalkeeper. He says he has springs in his heels, as well as sharp eyes and arms that stretch so he can reach a ball at the other side of the net. A magician, rather than a human being. If only his cousin Gilbert would stop bugging him about the swimming, Alfred would like these heated discussions at Sidi M'Cid to go on forever.

Auschwitz, Silesia, February 1944

'Get in the water, Nakache! Don't make us wait, all the staff are here to admire you, pal.'

Officer Müller, the man in charge of the Auschwitz infirmary building, is gloating. Nakache, the world record holder for the 200 metres breaststroke, is his favourite source of entertainment, along with the French boxer Victor Perez, the youngest ever flyweight world champion, known to everyone here as Young Perez or Younkie. Alfred stretches as he slowly gets up from his straw mattress, and pulls on his swimming trunks and his pyjamas under the mocking gaze of Müller and his two flunkies.

'Put this round your shoulders, it's not very warm outside,' he says, holding out a blanket.

Alfred doesn't like his smile. Ingratiating yet oozing contempt.

Just like last week, he finds himself standing shivering by the pool, with its dirty brown water covered with a layer of green algae. This pool is one of three reservoirs, each around fifteen metres long by six metres wide, scattered around the camp for fighting fires. The cold floods through him, freezing his bones, just like his anger at being there, a mere puppet of his torturers, the pathetic toy officers in immaculate uniforms. One of them is holding a stopwatch, the other a camera.

Obersturmführer Schwartz, the dreaded commandant of Auschwitz III, is rubbing his hands with glee. Gather round, ladies and gentlemen, the show's about to start!

'This time, Alfred my boy, you're going to give it everything. Ten lengths of butterfly. If you get below your previous time, you'll be allowed a bit of meat. If not, we'll save another of our specialities for you. A surprise, Alfred my boy, a surprise . . .'

Alfred knows what the punishment will be: the end of the comfort of the infirmary, back to the barracks, the darkness, the overcrowding, the disgusting soups. Back to those unbearable screams that pierce the night and penetrate the walls.

'Are you ready, champ?'

Save your skin, think only of yourself, not them. They don't exist. You're going to swim, Alfred, isolating yourself completely in the way you can. Your arms fully extended, your mouth open.

A shot rings out and he's in, his head already above the water, bringing up disgusting masses of vegetation. He hears laughter dissolving in his ears. He thrusts his shoulders even higher into the icy air. He hurts his pelvis with every stroke, gaining speed at every turn. *I'm swimming, dammit, I'm swimming well and to hell with them.*

'Well, Alfred, my boy, what do you reckon?' yells the general.

He doesn't answer, waiting, with his icy hands on the concrete. He can see them conferring, still smiling, again and again.

'Same time, my friend. We're going to need a second test to decide.'

When it comes to humiliation, their imagination knows no bounds. One officer pulls a knife from its sheath and holds it up in the air, beaming.

'It's going to be the dagger test, Alfred. Come and join us.'

Alfred gets out of the water, chilled to the bone. With his arms folded across his chest, he approaches his executioners.

'Well now,' says Schwartz triumphantly, 'we're going to throw this dagger into the middle of the pool. The tank is deep, but we know how talented you are. The game is to fetch it and bring it back up in your mouth. The knife between your teeth, got it, Alfred? What a great test! Like a doggie bringing it back to its master, you'll open your mouth and drop it at our feet. At least we hope so, you little rascal.'

Alfred estimates the pool to be at least six metres deep. That doesn't scare him, his lungs can cope with that. What worries him is the thick, opaque water that makes it impossible to see anything. It'll be like looking for a needle in a haystack. He has no choice but to give them this sadistic pleasure. Like all the detainees in the camp, he's at their mercy, a slave to their desire to destroy. Even so, he's lucky enough to have titles and medals, international recognition that makes him less transparent, less vulnerable. It's up to him to live up to his privileged status. The 'knife between the teeth' test, in a swamp, with a water temperature of ten degrees Celsius.

When the officer throws the dagger, he tries to follow its trajectory and identify its point of impact. Slightly towards the left, he thinks, two thirds of the way across the pool. He looks at the general, as if asking for permission to go ahead. With a ridiculous gesture, a kind of bow, the man invites him to jump into the water. He dives in immediately, swimming just below the surface, and heads to where he thinks the knife ended up. Then he dives straight down into the abyss, descending into the unknown. Long, interminable seconds pass, until the moment when his palms hit the hard, slimy bottom of the pool.

He raises his head, can't see further than a metre. He starts to feel his way over the ground, bumps into a pile of bricks, identifies what seems to be a trowel, gropes around as methodically as possible, in front, behind, to the right, to the left, while holding his breath. *Where's the bloody knife? They must be having a good laugh up there, maybe they think I'm already unconscious or half dead.* He's scrabbling around blindly now, with ever wider arm movements, and at last, with the tip of a finger, he feels the prick of a sharp point. He stretches out his arm and seizes hold of the object – the knife, with a blade at least twenty centimetres long. They'll get what they want, their photo of the bolshie with the knife between his teeth. Maybe, with a bit of luck, there will be some blood dripping from his lips, like you see on the posters.

He kicks as hard as he can to get back up to the surface and surges out of the water like an angry shark. The Nazi photographer bombards him with camera flashes, while the general jumps up and down like a child, applauding loudly. He spits out the knife. He's not bleeding. A soldier heaves him out of the water. He stands up, stumbling, exhausted. As he recovers, he sees them walk away and pile into their shiny Mercedes. For them, the show is over. As they are moving off, the *Obersturmführer* lowers the window and yells: 'Congratulations, Nakache. You'll be allowed some small meatballs in your soup tonight.' And with a bark of laughter, he adds: 'Make the most of it. Next week it'll be a different story.'

Alfred wraps himself in a blanket, unable to think, as though what just happened was nothing to do with him. It takes him a long time to start moving. Slowly he walks past the sinister barracks on his way back to the infirmary. A deathly silence surrounds him.

Sidi M'Cid swimming pool, May 1929

His cousins and his brothers would never have helped him conquer his fear of the water, let alone learn to love swimming enough to become one with the water. That small miracle happened on this day in May thanks to a training session for some French soldiers – ten or so strapping young men who had already mastered the four swimming strokes and, most importantly, looked radiant with happiness. So effort doesn't preclude pleasure after all, quite the opposite: you can suffer, push past your limits and feel a sort of exaltation. That day, Alfred watches their supple bodies cleaving the water, creating regular waves of white foam, as though taking part in a perfectly synchronized dance routine, embracing the immensity of the sky with every breath.

He's impressed by their tumble turns. They get so close to the wall, disappear in a flash as if they'd crashed into it head-first, then come up again faster than ever. At the end of the race, clinging to the starting blocks, they throw their arms round each other, congratulate each other, sometimes seem to be teasing each other. Rose often says that someone is 'happy as a fish in water' and now he understands this expression – even just sitting beside the pool, he feels in his element. Is it because he can't stop staring when one of the soldiers beckons him to dive in? Alfred answers with a shy shake of his head. No, not now. The soldier insists, and is joined by his friends.

'Come on, lad, the pool's all yours!' he yells.

Alfred doesn't move; he's petrified with fear. The young man swims a couple of strokes closer.

'What's your name?'

'Alfred.'

'Can't you swim?'

'A bit. Well, yes, I've learned to swim, but I'm not very keen on big swimming pools.'

'Small or large, it makes no difference, just keep to the edge of the pool and show me how you swim. You'll be fine. I'm Fabien, I'm the captain of the Algerian army swim team. We're staying here in Constantine for ten days, and then it's the big event: the Military Olympics in Algiers, ten countries competing.'

Surprised by his own boldness, or maybe just in order to gain some time, Alfred asks: 'Are you in with a chance?'

'Of course. In France, we have the best clubs in Europe, maybe in the world. Paris, Marseille, Toulouse, so many homes of future champions! Especially Toulouse, my club ever since I was little. Before joining the army and being sent to Algeria, I used to train there up to four times a week. Come on, it's your turn now.'

Fabien holds out a hand to pull him into the water.

'I'll swim beside you, start off slowly.'

Alfred lets go of the wall and starts swimming the crawl like a panicking dog, a series of jerky strokes with his mouth open, which makes him choke. Fabien stops him and brings him back to the edge of the pool.

'Calm down, Alfred! You're strong for your age, you're actually quite powerful, I can tell, but the engine's idling, you're exhausting yourself for nothing. Your arms aren't going far enough into the water and your legs aren't working. Watch me.'

He demonstrates in slow motion the incredibly long strokes that make him glide over the surface of the water. Alfred repeats those movements, trying to imitate the images recorded in his brain. He doesn't know if he's imagining it, but he feels he's reaching further, that his heart isn't pounding as hard and his breathing isn't letting him down. Here's hoping Fabien doesn't ruin this feeling with a crushing comment.

'That's right, there you go, that's good.'

Alfred hears these simple, reassuring words. Fabien's presence and his encouragement inspire him with a confidence he thought was beyond him. He's swimming with a champion who calmly pulls him along in his wake and he's no longer scared. He feels good. Very good, even. Like a fish, as Rose would say. That evening, he went to bed earlier than usual. With the window open, lulled by the sound of the cicadas, he imagined himself in Algiers, ready to dive into the pool in front of stands packed with overexcited supporters. His brother came into his room to tease him, as he did every evening. Alfred threw him out with unusual determination. In his dreams, it wasn't Fabien the military champion being applauded, but Alfred Nakache, the great new hope of French swimming. The unknown who used to tremble at the idea of entering the water and who is now getting ready to mount the podium. *B'ezrat Hashem*, as his father says. With God's help . . .

Constantine, April 1930

No one at home would have thought that Fabien's lessons would transform him so quickly. In the pool, Alfred swims length after length of freestyle without even lifting his head out of the water, sometimes for over an hour at a time.

'Oi! Alfred! Did you get some kind of jab or what?' sniggers his cousin as he turns at the end of a length.

Gilbert is lying on the starting block, with his mouth half in the water to make sure that Alfred can clearly hear his jeering comments. He might as well be talking to a brick wall. Alfred ignores him, determined to become a great swimmer. Never mind if they think he's a fool. In fact, he doesn't know exactly where this stubbornness bordering on pig-headedness comes from. Or rather yes, he thinks he does know: he needs people to believe in him and to say so, very loudly. When they do, he loses all his inhibitions. At school, at the Lycée d'Aumale, it's the same: he's only good at a subject if his teacher pays him plenty of attention. When

Madame Cherki, his history teacher, looks at him kindly, he's third-best in the class. When Monsieur Bardet, his maths teacher, glumly gives him back his marked homework, Alfred is second from the bottom. He sometimes wonders if he would have been different if he'd had an older brother, or a father who paid more attention to people's feelings and was less of a slave to his religion. Maybe Alfred needed more expressions of love than other people, and more admiration. He loves to admire people. It's like an engine inside him. He admires Fabien and in return, he wants Fabien to admire him. That's all there is to it. As Monsieur Bardet would say: 'It's not rocket science, for God's sake!'

One thing is for sure: this is all Alfred needs to make him feel strong and happy. It's enough to sweep away the doubts that surface too often, which he hides as best he can by playing the clown. That's what makes things difficult for his family and friends: he smiles all the time, whether he's deliriously happy or down in the dumps. It's not easy to find out which. At least he doesn't bore them with his moods. In the space of only a few weeks, he feels his adolescent body transforming. His shoulders are broader. In the mirror, his torso looks more and more like the pictures of Greek and Roman statues in his history book. His abdomen has developed a series of ridges, the outlines of which can be seen from the other end of the pool. As for his thighs, thanks to practising leg kicks he no longer has reason to envy the muscular legs of the Red Star footballers. He has legs like a carthorse. The only threat to Alfred's fitness are the warm, chocolate-covered rolls that his grandmother has baked especially for him in the communal oven, opposite the synagogue of Sidi-Fredj, which he wolfs down greedily when he returns from his training sessions.

Paule, July 1930

At the Sidi M'Cid pool, Alfred is basking in the sun after swimming dozens of lengths when he catches sight of her large green eyes. Irises sparkling with gold, almost too beautiful to be real. 'Like golden sequins', he says to himself. Paule Zaoui, the daughter of a Constantine cloth manufacturer, one of the most famous people in the Kar Chara, the Jewish quarter. Like Alfred, she is a pupil at the Lycée d'Aumale. Brilliant, solitary and unattainable, she accumulates distinctions and honours. The boys steer clear of her. She's too beautiful, too mysterious. She often comes to the pool with her brothers and sisters.

That day, she puts her towel down a few metres away from him. He pretends not to notice her figure, least of all her breasts, which he guesses are soft and firm, arousing in him a disturbing emotion. She appears to be trying to find the best position for sunbathing – on her stomach, on her back, with her legs straight or bent, and now on her side facing him, turning her large eyes towards his frightened face. Because he too is now lying on his side, with his head clumsily buried in his strong arms. She stands up, moves her towel another good metre closer, as if an approaching shadow was threatening to cover her legs.

'Paule!' He sputters out her name without even realizing.

'Oh, it's you, Alfred! I saw you in the water just now. How fast you swim! Everyone in the Zaoui family is talking about you. They say you're going to be a great champion.'

'I don't know about that, Paule.'

'Well, we know already,' she smiles, stretching out on her stomach. 'You're the fastest swimmer in Sidi M'Cid. Nobody can catch you.'

'What about you, do you like to swim?'

'I love diving. Anyway, that's enough sun for now, don't you think? Come and cool down.'

Before he has time to respond, she runs over to the pool and dives in, as graceful as a dancer. In a single bound, Alfred joins her. There they are, face to face, under the burning sun, in the blue pool with the rocky cliffs of the Rhumel gorge reflected in it. Alfred kicks with his feet to keep his torso upright and his shoulders out of the water. Paule hardly moves. She seems to float as she smooths back her hair and twists an elastic band round it, uncovering her broad, tanned forehead.

'Would you like to come to the cinema with me? They're showing *Sous les toits de Paris* at the Cirta. My cousins have been to see it, they say the songs are fantastic. And I would so like to see Paris . . .'

'Yes! Next Saturday?'

'Next Saturday.'

She takes a single stroke and throws her arms round his neck as if they had known each other forever. Alfred is dumbfounded by this speedy move. He's paralysed, incapable of making the slightest movement. The touch of Paule's skin sends shivers through his whole body. *Could this be falling in love?* He'd like to be brave enough to turn his head, meet her gaze, press his lips to hers, but he can't, it's all happening too fast. And after all, he's not sure about anything. Maybe she just wants to be his friend. The girlfriend of a future great swimmer. *Hide his anxiety. Relax in her embrace*. Rather than risking a hesitant kiss that might go horribly wrong, he suggests a game.

'Grab hold of my feet, with your arms stretched.'

Paule immediately twists round, grasps his ankles and says she's ready. And off they go across the Olympic pool, with him like a locomotive propelled by the strength of his arms and her like a train carriage firmly coupled to it. The faster he swims, the more she laughs, her voice clear and bright, like sparks of happiness that echo from the steep walls of the Rhumel and die away beyond the gorge.

The Toulouse–Paris train,
10 January 1944

The women who aren't handcuffed slip letters through the tops of the carriage windows, as if they were dropping a message in a bottle into the sea. The letters whirl around alongside the train, their crazy flight coming to an end wherever it may be – in the trees, under the tyres of a car or in the middle of a road, somewhere obvious enough for a charitable hand to pick it up and safely send it on its way. These letters express anxiety about the outcome of a journey under guard, they send words of love and encouragement, or sometimes just advice to wrap up warm against the winter cold. Premonitions of a journey with no return, urgent but unspecified appeals for help.

'I can't write very well, please help me,' begs Chaja, Paule and Alfred's neighbour.

Like Paule, this woman has a child in her arms. Her husband is firmly handcuffed at the other end of the carriage. Originally from a small village in Poland, Chaja and Zelman fled from the Nazis and found refuge in Haute-Garonne, in the south-west of France – part of the *zone libre*, the 'free zone' that was not under German occupation – where he worked as a tailor, and she as a nanny. Then the German invasion of the *zone libre* plunged them back into uncertainty and danger.

Paule reassures her, taking pains to write a few sentences to the family Chaja had worked for in Toulouse. Chaja was alone at the house in the Rue Saint-Louis when two militiamen came for her. She knew how kind the couple, both of them doctors, she worked for were. She knew that, if need be, they would be able to alert her husband's older brother, who had set up home further south, near Carcassonne. Paule writes the address as clearly as possible. Alfred, who had been spared being handcuffed, looks on in wonder as his wife acts with the kindness that captivated him right from the start. Having found her again, her and their little daughter Annie, after the violence of their arrest and then their separation in the Saint-Michel prison in Toulouse, is already a victory. Everyone on this train, which hundreds of people boarded in Toulouse, recognizes Alfred's face. Nakache is still a star, despite his recent absence from the pool. They look at him with admiration, sometimes with embarrassment. *Why is he on this journey too?* Even the French policemen who come across him are ill at ease.

One young man has no such qualms. His name is Léon.[1] He's twenty-three, and he's accompanied by Louise, his older sister, who is sitting in the front of the carriage. On the day of her arrest, acting on instinct, Louise managed to save her five-year-old daughter by pretending she was the child of the concierge. Now she knows her daughter is safe.

Léon approaches the champion.

'I'm delighted to be able to talk to you. I've been following all your records for two years,' he says with a smile. 'The Germans have gone mad.'

'What about you, what do you do?' Alfred asks.

'I was a switchboard operator in Toulouse, but they gave me the sack. Since then, I've been doing small electrical jobs, here and there. I get by all right. Before that, I was just a little *poulbot*.'

'A *poulbot*? What's that?'

'A Montmartre street urchin, if you prefer. That's where I learned to sing. I spend my life singing. Some people pray when things are going badly, some people cry, others keep silent. I sing!'

'You're absolutely right to do that, my friend! What about your parents, where are they?'

'Still in Paris.'

'Isn't that too dangerous?'

'They have a little fabric shop right opposite the police station in the 18th arrondissement. The superintendent decided to protect them; I've no idea why. My parents trust him and have never registered themselves as Jewish. Maybe the superintendent is impressed by my father's life story: a Romanian who joined the French army in the trenches, a convinced socialist, a naturalized Frenchman, the father of five children . . . and he hasn't a penny to his name!'

'It's possible,' says Alfred, as the train slows down again and stops.

'I'll take the first opportunity to scarper,' whispers Léon, looking all around him. 'But my sister Louise never stops repeating, *I can't run, I can't run* . . . It was such a shambles at the Matabiau station back in Toulouse that we could have got away then.'

'Don't take any risks, Léon. And look after Louise.'

The Toulouse–Paris train is a proper local train. It crawls along for twenty-four hours on its way to the Gare d'Austerlitz in Paris. On the platform, as day is only just beginning to break, the police escort the detainees to dozens of requisitioned buses. Where are they going? Nobody knows.

The Parisians on their way to work don't seem to suspect anything, or be worried about anything.

Last stop before Pitchipoi

Standing on the open platform at the back of the bus, Alfred has just enough time to see the name of the place: Drancy. It's about fifteen kilometres north of Paris. This outer suburb means nothing to him. Before he left for Toulouse, the big swimming pools of Paris were where he defied the stopwatches.

The column of buses slowly crosses the town, then stops with a noise of grinding metal that makes their exhausted bodies jump. Alfred leans over the side. A few metres away is a group of greyish buildings in what looks like a horseshoe shape, surrounded by a barbed wire fence. French policemen with rifles slung over their shoulders are on guard. A murmuring sound that Alfred hears coming from behind the walls is getting louder. It's the sound of a noisy crowd, punctured by orders shouted in German, sharp cries and the voices of women singing that seem to rise heavenward. The bus gives another shake. With Paule and Annie, Alfred enters this place, which looks unfinished. Four-storey dwellings with neither windows nor doors, open to the icy wind, crammed with probably over a thousand people – men, women, children and the elderly.

Drancy. A concrete residential estate transformed into an internment camp, with five fourteen-storey tower blocks looming over it – the first skyscrapers to be built in France. It's impossible to imagine that the Cité de la Muette was once meant to be a model of urban development – a social utopia that, according to its developer Henri Sellier, was going to provide 'better housing for humanity, aiming for a level of light, joy, health . . . ' Inside, no more policemen, but Nazis and bossy henchmen appointed from among the detainees to allocate spaces, assign activities and maintain order by means of insults and truncheons. The stench is unbearable, as is the dirt on the ground and the walls. Relieving yourself without authorization is prohibited. Moving for no purpose is prohibited. So people do what they can.

Léon the electrician sees his sister Louise being pushed to the other end of the camp. He is taken to a building close to the Nakaches, who have been lucky enough to be able to stay together. Once again, people approach Alfred, recognizing the great champion whose picture has been in the papers so often. In the room they have been allotted, Alfred observes two boys who stick to each other like glue. Two brothers with very different expressions. The first one, the younger of the two, has laughing eyes. His name is Gérard,[2] he's barely sixteen, a short, sturdy lad, full of energy. The older one, Pierre, is a beanpole with small round spectacles that allow all his melancholy to be seen. Unlike Gérard, who keeps staring at Alfred, Pierre doesn't seem to recognize the swimmer. He's not looking at anyone, for that matter, just staring down at the ground.

Alfred gets up and offers the two boys a piece of chocolate. Gérard is thrilled to find himself face to face with Nakache, but has no problem expressing his admiration for him. He tells him that they arrived from Marseille a few days before, with his mother and his sister Mireille, but have had no more news of them. As for their father, he was arrested two weeks earlier at his import agency for products from Algeria. He was the first person, Gérard says, to have ordered Moses baskets for babies. It was sheer madness in the Vieux-Port of Marseille. Since then, there's been no news of him either.

'I'm from Algeria too,' whispers Alfred. 'From Constantine, to be precise. That's where I learned to swim.'

'My father worships you. Two years ago, when you broke the world record for the 200 metres breaststroke in Marseille, he wasn't able to be there at the pool, but he treasured the newspaper article with the photo where you stuck your tongue out.'

'It's a habit of mine,' says Alfred with a smile.

'Do you know what they're planning to do with us?'

'Not the slightest idea.'

'The old people say we're going to pick strawberries in Alsace. Or that we're going to Pitchipoi.'

'Pitchipoi?'

'The country that doesn't exist,' an old man sitting next to them against the wall suddenly says with a sigh.

The country that doesn't exist . . . Alfred's blood runs cold. Paule is focused on taking care of Annie. Until now, the few supplies she brought with her have been enough to ease her daughter's hunger, but the days pass, colder and colder, and the lack of hygiene leaves its mark on their bodies.

★ ★ ★

In the courtyard at Drancy, where the shouts of the SS and their henchmen shatter the eardrums like hammer blows on a sheet of iron, Alfred sees Léon approaching, a determined look on his face. He has oval goggles on his forehead, a toolbox in his hand and an armband saying 'electrician' around his arm.

'I've managed to pass myself off as an electrical engineer. I said I'd studied at the engineering school. The SS officer believed me, he seemed to know it. He looked delighted. I lay cables to supply the guardhouse at the entrance. This time, I'm going to get out.'

'But what about your sister, Léon?'

'Louise? I found out that they put her on a train the day after we arrived. I've got nothing left to lose.'

Alfred says nothing. It's difficult to counter such rage. Léon heads off again with a steady stride, toolbox in hand, giving Alfred a confident thumbs up.

★ ★ ★

Every evening, in the windowless room they share with many other detainees, Alfred, Paule and Annie huddle together on the hard, damp floor to find a little warmth. The soup they are given is disgusting, a yellowish liquid with a few potato peelings floating in it. What with the draughts, the smell, the mould and the electric lights in the yard that shine all night long, sleep is slow in coming. Many of them write to ward off the anguish of this suspended time with no end in sight.

There are some everyday messages: *'I forgot to close the shutters. Take the kid's coat.'* Some are words of love: *'I miss you, my darling wife, don't worry about me . . .'* Others are cheerful, amusing letters like those of Louise Jacobson or Gabriel Ramet: *'I got your parcel. Ah! What a feast . . . Thank you from the bottom of my heart and stomach.'* There are words of great sorrow, like this anonymous letter, simply signed: *'The suffering woman, and my kids.'*[3]

As for Alfred, he has got into the habit of quietly talking with Gérard. He likes this young lad who always has his big brother's back. In the middle of the night, they talk about Marseille and Constantine. About the sun that keeps growing fainter.

'I was shocked when the Boches blew up the Vieux-Port and the transporter bridge,' says Gérard. 'For the first time, we were frightened, but it didn't stop us from taking our trips to the coast at Sormiou or Morgiou, or going to the Parc Borély to see the bullfights and boxing matches.'

'Do you remember any fights in particular?'

'Yes, Marcel Cerdan knocking out Frely in the third round. Fernand Frely. A Swiss boxer.'

'What about swimming?'

'Last summer, we went to the Chevalier-Roze pool every weekend. But that wasn't our real passion. What we liked was eating *frigolosi* on the beach, the best kind of ices.'

'One day I'll tell you about the lemon sorbets my grandmother used to make in Constantine . . .'

Amid the boredom and the fear, these stolen snatches of conversation are like acid drop sweets that help them keep going. But they also make the hunger and the dirt even more distressing. Touching his cheeks that are covered with untidy bristles, transforming his face into an unruly wasteland, and looking at his filthy hands and the damp clothes that are going mouldy on his body, Alfred is overcome with disgust. And with sorrow for Paule, who still looks presentable, but only with tremendous effort. *Never,* he says to himself, *would I have believed that you could get louse-ridden in such a short time.*

* * *

— 29 —

In Drancy, on 17 January 1944, Alfred is summoned to the offices of Aloïs Brunner, who has been the dreaded commandant of the camp since the previous June.[4] Around Brunner, a dozen or so subordinate SS officers, all Austrians like him, serve as his inner circle. Alfred is received by *Oberscharführer* Joseph Weiszl, a former hairdresser in Vienna. The staff officer explains that in view of his considerable sporting achievements, Alfred will be able to return to Toulouse.

'Unfortunately,' he says, 'we can't do anything for your wife and daughter.'

'That's a no, then,' says Alfred.

'Think about it, Monsieur Nakache.'

'I've thought about it.'

'Have it your own way,' the officer says in a sarcastic tone and abruptly dismisses him from the room.[5]

Two days later, Alfred learns that the next morning they will be taken to the train station in Bobigny, a few kilometres from the camp. The craziest theories about this new transfer spread around the courtyard and through the buildings. While most people look apprehensive, some cling to the hope of a brighter future. Haven't they been promised that this time they wouldn't be handcuffed? That they would be able to leave with all their luggage? That they would be given enough food for several days? Gérard is the first to be willing to see some encouraging signs. His brother Pierre, however, is very nervous, and as silent as always.

At about 10pm, a few minutes before the roll-call that requires everyone to go back to their rooms, Alfred and Paule are repacking their travel bag, cramming in as much as possible, when Léon suddenly appears, wearing his electrician's armband.

'I'm leaving with you tomorrow.'

'How come?' Alfred asks in astonishment.

Despite all his attempts, Léon hasn't managed to escape. The SS have been on edge after discovering a secret tunnel through which dozens of detainees have escaped. Léon wasn't on the list for the next convoy – the Nazis are in need of his skills as an electrician to improve the lighting in the camp – but he has insisted on his name being added.

'On the train, without Louise, I'll be able to escape.'

'You're mad . . . What have you told them?'

'That I was accompanying a girlfriend.'

'Who is this girl?'

'I met her yesterday. She was lying in the corner of the entrance to one of the buildings, in tears. She told me that all her family had already been taken away and now it was her turn to go. I comforted her by saying we'd get the train together. I don't know anything about her.'

Léon the *poulbot*, the Montmartre street urchin. The last one to join the train for Pitchipoi.

Convoy 66

20 January 1944. The journey is appalling. Stifling. Crammed into a cattle truck, they are plunged into complete darkness. They can hardly make out so much as a ray of light between the planks of the sliding door. Very soon they are plagued by thirst. Their throats are dry, and it feels as if their lips are swelling and their tongues hardening. The next day, there is a stink of urine and excrement everywhere, disgraceful, as if they were animals. There are over a thousand of them.[6] Alfred doesn't let go of Paule's hand, as she clutches Annie tightly in her arms. Annie, who had her cuddly toy, a little black dog, snatched from her before they left. Annie, who's just two years old.

What can they say to their little daughter? That it's nothing – just a bad moment that won't last too long, but I swear, I promise, you can believe Mum and Dad, all this will soon come to an end. Tomorrow there will be daylight. Tomorrow the golden rays of the sun will make the vast plain of Pitchipoi sparkle and Annie will be able to have her first snowball fight there.

Three days and two nights. *Around them, children cry, parents pray, the sick and elderly groan* . . . Three days and two nights of the stench, the fear and the unbearable heat of bodies sticking to one another in an airless space. Suddenly the axles of the train start to squeal. The train brakes, brakes again, then stops abruptly. It's the night of 22–23 January. In the distance they can hear the barking of dogs and the voices of approaching German soldiers. With a deafening crash, the doors of the wagon slide fully open. The icy wind lashes their skin, the white glare of the huge searchlights aimed at their sleeping bodies burns their eyes. Alfred doesn't know what time it is – no one has had a watch since they left Drancy – but it must be between midnight and one in the morning.

'Faster! Come on, get down on the platform, faster!' yells an SS officer, whose orders mingle with the growls of the overexcited dogs.

Alfred grabs Paule's hand, helps her to jump down, while exhausted elderly people collapse on the frozen platform. The soldiers push away anyone who tries to help them up. Some will die here, right in front of them. Moaning in despair, they hold out their hands to their children. Alfred watches them tenderly, his eyes and a forced smile offering all the love he has in him, but the officer is already jostling him and tearing his hand away from Paule's.

'Her and the child, to the right, *rechts*, you, to the left, *links*. Faster!'

Now they're in two columns, separated by a few metres that seem like an abyss. Their eyes are drawn to one another as if they were making love, they talk to each other, knowing that neither of them can make out the slightest sound in this chorus of shouts and tears. Their cracked lips form impossible words. Alfred is pushed forward again. Men are being manhandled towards the left-hand column. A soldier examines him, murmurs something to his superior, who comes over. He's lost sight of Paule and Annie. He has the impression that they've been directed to a covered lorry.

'You're Nakache, is that correct?' asks the officer.

'Yes, sir. *Ich bin Nakache. Ich bin ein Schwimmer.*'

'The great champion Nakache, what a pleasure it is to welcome you here! You look in pretty good shape after that long journey.'

Alfred forces a smile while his stomach churns with rage. He would like to grab him by the throat, make this stupid bastard repeat his sugary words while he pulls his starched collar tight around his neck, tears off his swastika and forces him to eat it. But the officer has already gone.

'You're lucky, mate,' whispers a little man aged about forty, with a southern French accent and a grey suit that's too short for him. In the middle of all the chaos, this man appears to be remaining calm. 'They're going to make us work.'

'But what about my wife and daughter?'

The man lowers his eyes a little and takes Alfred by the shoulder. 'Don't think about it, nobody knows. The best thing you can do is make yourself useful. They need us. What are they called, your wife and daughter?'

'Paule and Annie.'

'And what about you?'

'Alfred.'

'You'll find them again, Alfred.'

He doesn't have time to ask the man's name before he is pushed towards a lorry. The vehicle travels some ten kilometres over chaotic roads, passes a small town called Monowitz, then stops at the entrance to a camp. In the distance, in the semi-darkness, Alfred sees the smoking chimneys of a gigantic factory. *Is that where they're going to send us to work?*

Auschwitz – First day

'Undress!' shout the SS guards.

Like all the others, Alfred takes off his clothes and stands stark naked in the snow, which is falling in large flakes. Naked in a temperature of minus twenty degrees Celsius, shivering from head to toe, his hands covering his exposed private parts. Waiting for hours for something to happen. *But what . . .?* A few rows away, an SS guard walks past Léon and fetches him a violent blow to the face with the butt of his rifle.

'He's crazy!' the enraged electrician says, trying to wipe away the blood with his hand.

A detainee to Léon's right turns towards him: 'No, they said "naked" and you kept your glasses on.'

Then the door of the barracks opposite them suddenly opens.

'Inside, *schnell*!' barks the block-leader.

The detainees are ordered to climb on benches. Some men appear with electric trimmers. Their task is to shave the detainees all over: legs, genitals, chest, armpits, head, eyebrows. When shaving their heads, they leave a strip of stubble in the centre. The Germans call it *'the Autobahn'* . . . Then they are ordered to go back outside and head over to another block of huts. This one is divided in two: on one side, the steam room, with pipes spewing burning-hot vapour; on the other, the ice room. This hot-and-cold treatment lasts for hours and is supposed to cleanse their bodies of all parasites, to avoid the spread of typhus. Some people can't handle it. Their corpses are thrown into lorries.

In front of Alfred and the other detainees, the *Blockältester*, the block-leader, climbs on a stepladder. He's wearing a tight-fitting black suit and looks in good shape. The two hundred detainees are still stark naked. The leader whispers something in his deputy's ear. The man comes back with a leather-covered truncheon and a huge spade. The leader beckons to one of the detainees to leave the line and come over. The poor devil, chosen at random, does as he's told. As soon as he reaches the boss's feet, truncheon blows rain down on him. Not one, but three, five, ten – blows so violent that the guy collapses. The *Blockältester* gets down from the stepladder, lets go of the truncheon and grabs the big spade. He places the long handle across the man's throat, and puts a foot on either side of his head. Then he starts rocking to and fro, throttling the poor guy who is lying on the ground, moaning. The moaning soon stops. Total silence. Léon and the other prisoners no longer dare to breathe. They have just witnessed their first murder. The *Blockältester* gets up and gives back the tools. He explains, as if any explanation were needed, that he's the boss. He can kill them all, one after the other. He has the right to do this.

Once again, they trudge through the snow for several hundred metres. Jabs in the arm await them. Needles dipped in ink that mark out a six-figure number, an indelible tattoo. A mark of infamy displayed forever on their bruised skin. The tattooist on duty soon recognizes Nakache. Nakache, the champion, nameless from now on. Reduced to a number: 172763. The tattooist wishes him all the best – without animosity, with a kind of amused curiosity. On leaving, they are all directed towards a mountain of old pyjamas that have previously been worn by others. Striped pyjamas, black with grime and traces of excrement caused by dysentery. They are also given a cap and a pair of wooden clogs, often not a matching pair. No shirts, underpants or socks. Nothing but this piece of rough, dirty fabric to protect them from the winter and the interminable roll-calls. Once he's dressed again, Alfred is pulled out of the column by an officer.

'You're a sturdy fellow and people recognize you. We're going to assign you to the central infirmary to serve Professor Waitz. He's from Alsace, a leading expert in medicine. He's in charge of the dispensary in block 18. You'll get on splendidly.'

At that moment, Alfred knows he will escape the worst. In his group of detainees, people start chatting during this endless wait. Prisoners assigned to snow-clearing duty have been able to talk to some of those on the road, braving the watchful eyes of the guards. They describe disgusting barracks, stacks of louse-infested bedsteads, a refuge for rats, mites and cockroaches. A single slop bucket. No light, not a breath of air. Nauseating soup. People die there every day from exhaustion and malnutrition; their bodies are removed like animal carcasses and thrown into skips to be burned somewhere out of sight. So that's what those tall chimneys spewing black smoke into the spotless blue sky are. Furnaces. Crematoria. There would be three of them. As they walk past the blocks, everyone gets a mouthful of this nauseating, sour taste. The vile green smell of death.

In an expressionless voice, Élie, a man of about sixty, with a clear gaze and skinny arms, tells Alfred and those around him that whole groups of Jews are being sent to the gas chambers here at the Auschwitz camp before being reduced to ashes. How come he's so sure? He explains that until two years ago, he was the chief engineer in charge of roads and public works in Paris. After being expelled from the administration, he kept in touch with one of the advisers to the Minister of Infrastructure and Transport, who warned him several times: 'You escaped the big Vél' d'Hiv' round-up[7], but the police are now clearing the whole area, including the *zone libre* south of the Loire. All the arrested Jews are taken to Drancy and then by special trains to the camps in Germany or Poland, where they are systematically gassed.'

For a long time, Élie was hidden by a family of Catholic industrialists in Paris, in a building on the Rue de l'Université. In the end he was caught, knowing the fate that awaited him.

Alfred leaves Élie and this group of despondent men, their bodies already exhausted, who no longer seem to believe in anything. He watches them walk away in the dusk, not knowing if he'll ever see them again.

Paule and Annie, where are you? Where are you, my darlings? Alfred knows how strong Paule is, he knows she'll find words to comfort Annie, a way to mollify her torturers and stay alive. She and their child. She'll talk about him, yes, that's it: *I'm the wife of Alfred Nakache, you know, the great champion, the king of butterfly, she's his daughter, she looks so much like him, don't you think?* She'll also tell them that she's a gym teacher, that she can give lessons to the officers' wives that could be useful in this icy cold. Alfred is sure she's already told them. And that, thanks to her few words of German, they've understood.

He would so like to know which barrack they're in. This camp stretches further than the eye can see. Maybe she's been assigned to the IG-Farben factory, on the other side of the barbed wire? Élie told them about that too. The rubber factory employs men and women who are in good health. She's young, beautiful, energetic; they would certainly have spotted her. There would even be a gypsy orchestra playing to encourage the workers on their way to and from the factory. Tomorrow he'll ask Professor Waitz how to get news of them. First night in Auschwitz. First sleepless night, as empty as the frozen land all around them. The hours pass and his eyes are still wide open. Tiredness makes no difference, falling asleep is impossible. *What am I doing here in this hell? Daddy, what does God tell you?*

It's a mistake, of course. None of that is real. A mistake.

September 1931 – On your marks, get set . . .?

Every stopwatch bears witness to Alfred's transformation. His times improve day after day. At the Jeunesse Nautique Constantinoise, the swimming club that has become Alfred's second home, Gabriel Menut has no more doubts: the time for competitions has arrived.

'I'm putting you down for freestyle, in Algiers, in the North African championships!' Menut shouts as he helps him out of the pool. 'Not just to take part, but to win.'

'But I'm only sixteen, there'll be lots of people with more experience than I have.'

'You know the saying, young Alfred: *Aux âmes bien nées, la valeur n'attend point le nombre des années*. [In souls nobly born, worth does not wait for the number of years]. It's from a play by Corneille, I think.'

He's bluffing. On 5 September 1931, the entire Nakache clan has assembled along the sides of the Olympic pool. Even his father, David, has made the trip. The only person missing is Paule, with her radiant smile and her big green eyes. It's the moment of all hopes, all promises. Over the summer, Alfred has swum for more than three hours a day to make up for last term's lack of training. He only abstained from swimming for one day in mid-August, for the fast day of Tisha B'av, commemorating the fall of the Temple of Jerusalem. On that day, so Rose and all the local mothers assure him, the sea is infested with sharks and sharp knives. No question of taking the slightest risk, not even in the swimming pool.

The rest of the year, there is little space in his timetable. Like many Jewish children in Constantine, he attends lessons at the Alliance, the Hebrew school, on Thursday and Saturday mornings, in addition to his compulsory schooling at the Lycée d'Aumale. It's a religious school where everything has to be learned by heart – Hebrew, the prayers, the history of the Bible and Judaism – and the slightest infringement of the rules, the slightest sign of inattention, incurs corporal punishment, slaps, ear-pulling or, harsher still, being struck on the hands and the soles of the feet with a ruler, the dreaded *tcharmela*.

On the starting block, a few seconds before the start of the race, Alfred's knees are shaking. The pressure, the overpowering heat, the fear of losing. He shivers, glances anxiously towards his family, who respond with loud shouts of encouragement.

'Give it your all!' yells Prosper, who has come closer to the pool, with his elbows on the railings.

Alfred smiles, but his eyes betray the panic that has engulfed him. The crack of the pistol! He dives as far as he can. *One hundred metres freestyle, Alfred, just one hundred metres* . . . But his mind is blurry, getting lost in the churning water that has become hostile. When he strains his arms, he swallows a mouthful of water, first one then another, while a dull roar, tending towards the bass notes, rumbles in his ears. *What are they saying? . . . Where am I? . . . Where are the others? . . .* Alfred veers off course, he's out of his lane, blindly continuing to swim in a diagonal. Prosper puts his head in his hands. His father covers his eyes. The commentator hands down the sentence: 'Alfred Nakache, disqualified.' His first competition, and his first failure. Alfred stays at the end of the pool for a long time, alone and exhausted.

'We're going to work on your head together,' his coach says reassuringly, putting a bathrobe round Alfred's shoulders. 'You couldn't ask for a better lesson.'

On the way home, in the cross-country train on the Oujda-Oran-Alger-Constantine-Ghardimaou line, father and son don't speak to one another. The next day, when it's time for the anisette Phénix, the favourite aperitif of the inhabitants of Constantine, the men on the crowded terraces of the Rue de France describe what everyone in Kar Chara experienced as a cold shower. The local paper, *the Écho sportif du département de Constantine,* doesn't beat about the bush: 'The most anticipated race of the meet was spoiled by young Nakache's stupid blunder, changing lanes. What a fool!'

★ ★ ★

A few months later, Alfred gets a second chance. A sea race to be held on the day after Christmas in the bay of Philippeville, just under a hundred kilometres from Constantine. Four hundred metres freestyle in much rougher waters than at the Sidi M'Cid pool. On the Lido beach, below hills covered with centuries-old pines and cedars, the excitement is palpable. The high society of Algiers and Constantine has gathered along the beach to watch the traditional Constantine Christmas Cup.

In events of this kind, the advantage lies with the strong and sturdy, those who can deal with the heavy swell and play with the waves. It's no place for swimming with finesse. Alfred shouldn't say it, but this time, even before the start, he knows he has a race to win. He only needs to see the way the other swimmers are eyeing his biceps to be sure of it. Most importantly, he has learned his lesson. This time, he stays on course with military precision, doesn't bump into any buoys, ploughs conscientiously through the sea. His first victory – far from the pool, out in the open sea. Just like in his childhood dreams, he's thrust into the limelight.

This first title justifies all the hopes of the little wimp who used to tremble on his starting block in Algiers. The entire Nakache clan is stunned. Back at home, his little brothers jump up and down on their beds, holding up the trophy. You'd think they had their hands on the Jules-Rimet Cup, the new football World Cup that was won last year in Uruguay by the home team, nicknamed *La Celeste,* 'The Sky Blue'. His grandmother has prepared a banquet fit for a king: couscous with mutton and a cake elaborately decorated with nougatine. For the first time, Alfred feels the sheer joy you experience when you make people you love happy.

The music of Cheikh Raymond

Once a week in the summer of 1932, Paule and Alfred, their feet clad only in sandals, rush down through the alleyways of old Constantine and take the cliff road that plunges down into the gorge. At sunset, they head for one of the first bends in the road, with an amazing backdrop of rocks, waterfalls and greenery, where they have got into the habit of meeting a young Arab trader and treating themselves to the prickly pears he has picked. On each of these outings, they choose a fully ripe, orangey-red fruit from a basket lined with fresh leaves, picking it up with their bare hands, and with the point of a knife, they make the spiny skin expel the sweet, juicy pulp that mingles with the kisses they now regularly exchange in the shelter of the bushes, cacti and agaves.[8] Around them, myriads of little red adonis flowers pirouette in the gentle breeze. At Easter, these flowers, placed in a goblet of water, decorate the table. The Jews of Constantine call them 'drops of blood'. In the midst of this luxuriant nature, the overwhelming beauty of the cliffs split by the gorge, Paule and Alfred often linger late into the evening, sitting cross-legged, contemplating the mysterious moment when the sun disappears from the sky, sliding into the night and silence.[9]

That same summer, Alfred starts seeing a lot of Cheikh Raymond, three years his senior, the young prince of ma'luf music who delights Constantine with his Arab-Andalusian melodies. The musician has just been accorded the prestigious title of *cheikh* – 'grand master'. The two boys have known each other for a long time. They both attended the strict Alliance school, in the Rue Thiers, which instilled in them ambition, a work ethic, honesty and a sound knowledge of the sacred texts.

Above all, the two of them have in common the awed recognition that brings a gleam to the eyes of young and old – Raymond through music, Alfred in the swimming pool. They are listened to and idolized. Raymond's real name is Leyris, and his story is that of the city and its thousands of influences. Cheikh Raymond's father, Jacob Levi, is Jewish and his mother is from the south of France; she has a French name, Céline Leyris – and she sings in Arabic. She is loved by all, worshipped even as the inheritor and keeper of secrets of composition dating back to the far-off centuries of Andalusian grandeur. She is always ready to use her oud, the Arabian lute played in Constantine, and her warm voice to enchant the guests at weddings, bar mitzvahs and many other family ceremonies.

Cheikh Raymond had a job as a house painter, but this year, like Alfred, all his time is taken up by his passion. One of the places where Cheikh Raymond performs his repertoire is reserved for the initiated, a place where children are not welcome and it is frowned upon for a woman to venture: the *funduq*. In a book about Constantine, Alfred had read this surprising description: 'The *funduq* is both a hotel and a conservatoire, a caravanserai and a place to store goods, an oasis of high civilization and a cavern of passions, a place of perdition and a safe refuge.'[10] That evening, at the Café de Paris, Alfred, who is still only seventeen, wants to know more about these mysterious places.

'I learned everything at the Funduq Benazzouz,' Raymond tells him. 'I had just turned thirteen, I was one of the youngest there. I was listening to the great Abdelkrim Bestandji, the undisputed king of the oud. A man of passion, who would rather play all night for his friends than for two handsomely paid hours in the salon of a rich merchant.'

'Did he recognize a future talent in you? Is that why he accepted you?'

'It was probably just like it was with you, Alfred. One day you cross paths with someone, they believe in you and your life is changed forever.'

'What do you think he noticed first?'

'I don't know if it was my playing or my singing, maybe both. At Benazzouz, they said I was just as much at ease in the low and high registers, and for ma'luf, which expresses nostalgia and inner suffering, that's important.'

'Will you take me there?'

'More easily than you can take me to a pool,' he says, with a note of irony.

The following week, Alfred finds himself not at Benazzouz, but in the flower-filled courtyard of the Funduq Ben-Azéim. Under Raymond's benevolent gaze, he sits down discreetly in the shade of a fig tree, captivated by the timeless ambience in which his friend's songs and the notes of his lute vanish into the wreaths of hashish smoke. Around him, social outcasts on their last legs and notables from the suburbs unite around what Cheikh Raymond, at the grand age of twenty, likes to call a 'wonderful sorrow'. Alfred feels a bit out of place in this universe full of the melancholy and artificial paradises described by the 19th century poets, but he allows himself to be carried away. He closes his eyes, drifts gently into meditation, allows himself to be overcome by new emotions. *It's a bit like being in the water*, he thinks. In the water where, as only swimmers know, effort can make suffering feel close to ecstasy.

May 1944 – A travesty of a fight

In the middle of the courtyard of Auschwitz III, where the prisoners line up for roll-call, the SS have set up an almost perfect boxing ring, at the correct height and with impeccable ropes. Several dozen rows of chairs reserved for Nazi dignitaries surround the square where Victor Young Perez, the world flyweight champion, is preparing to fight one of the camp guards, a former amateur middleweight boxer, who is much bigger and stronger than he is – and above all, much better fed. Victor's opponent is trained by Kurt Magatans, an ordinary German prisoner, once a decent boxer, now serving a life sentence for three murders. Squatting or standing at the back, a handful of hand-picked detainees are watching this farcical match. Among them is Alfred, who shares the status of great international champion with Victor.

Like Alfred, Victor had no choice but to satisfy the whims of his torturers. He turns towards Alfred, who gives him a discreet wave of recognition – two French sports stars plunged into the absurd. Victor gears himself up to regain his fleet footwork of old. Get his opponent off balance, make him run, tire him out – against the burly German, he has no other option. While the officers relish the spectacle, Alfred can't take his eyes off Victor. The lad from Tunis no longer has the muscle tone he once did, his movements are stiffer, more jerky, but he occasionally manages to land a few hooks on the guard's ribs and make him wince.

One round follows another, without either of the boxers really gaining the upper hand. In Victor's case, Alfred senses that it's deliberate. There's no point in annoying men who have the power of life or death over him at any time. After twelve rounds, the referee declares a draw, to applause from the officers. A strange verdict, when it would be so easy to call a win. Victor wants to believe that this evening is a good omen, that his status as a champion is the best protection he has. On leaving the ring, he heads towards Alfred, excited to meet, even under these dire circumstances, the man who made the front page of the sports press so many times. They don't know each other but they hug for a long time.

'You have the same smile as on the cover of *Match*,' says Victor, like an old friend.

'I'd rather have met you in a bar in Montparnasse, but it is how it is. Bravo anyway for your performance, you kept the right distance. From all points of view!'

The two men stand to one side while the detainees get on with dismantling the ring amid the shouts of the guards. An officer watches them, as if he's wondering what they might be telling each other, but he doesn't intervene. Maybe he thinks they both deserve this little break. Leaning back against the wall surrounding the courtyard, Alfred and Victor begin a conversation that is as rambling as it is joyful. It's as if there were thousands of things they urgently needed to say to one another; as if time was running out. They talk about the lands of their childhoods – Tunisia and Algeria – their modest, hard-working families, the traditional celebrations that punctuate the lives of North-African Jews, the culture that unites them more than anything.

Strangely, on that day they don't say a word about their sporting lives, as if all that was in fact secondary. Alfred prefers to talk about meeting Cheikh Raymond, the prince of ma'luf, about how his songs are filled with nostalgia yet also with promises of life. He hums the tune of Raymond's song *Insraff Zidane*, and bursts out laughing.

'Sorry, I'm a lousy singer!'

Victor smiles in response, and his sad eyes light up with a spark of joy.

'Personally, what left the biggest mark on me as a child, was my father reading aloud from *The Count of Monte-Cristo*.'

'Monte-Cristo?'

'Yes, a story written by Alexandre Dumas.'

'The favourite author of my French teacher at the Lycée d'Aumale. But I've never read it.'

'Nor have I, don't worry, but on Shabbat evenings my father recited whole passages of it to us. He would wear his rust-coloured djellaba to mark the occasion.'

'What's it about?'

'A man at rock bottom, held captive in the Château d'If off the coast of Marseille, who seeks a way to freedom and happiness. Edmond Dantès, soon to become the Count of Monte-Cristo!'

'A bit like our story,' jokes Alfred, sadly.

'Why not, my friend? Listen, I know this bit by heart: "While Edmond Dantès was giving in to despair, from the next cell there came a kind of scratching. He listened and heard a faint voice. It was the abbé Faria."'

'His saviour?'

'In a way. The meeting that's about to change everything. Our father used to say: "You see, children, after anguish comes deliverance. Edmond's enemies thought they had destroyed him, but God took pity on him and worked a miracle to save him."'[11]

If only books were true, thinks Alfred as he stares at the barbed wire in the distance that keeps them imprisoned. He doesn't have time to reply to Victor before an officer orders them back to their barracks.

'We'll find a way to meet up again soon,' whispers Alfred.

'You can tell me a bit about boxing next time. And *mabrouk* – congratulations – on your performance!'

★ ★ ★

Miracles sometimes keep you waiting. A few weeks later, Victor, who is assigned to work in the kitchens, steals a bowl of soup full of vegetables and meat, so that he can secretly take it to a friend who is at the end of his strength. He has hardly got through the door when he's grabbed by the collar. The guard beats him violently with a club and, after a discussion with his superiors, throws him into a prison cell where he's left to rot for a fortnight, surrounded by a colony of rats. Victor loses his job in the kitchens, only just escapes *Selektion* – being sent to the gas chamber – and is assigned to an excavation squad.

After that, his health and morale steadily deteriorate. The Count of Monte-Cristo vanishes. The child of the souks is reduced to a shadow of his former self.

January 1933 – The big leap

It's snowing in Constantine, as it does every winter. This year it's bitterly cold, as hard to bear as the stifling summer heat in the apartments of Kar Chara, blasted by the sirocco. From the wrought-iron balconies and the terraces overlooking the buildings, the children engage in endless snowball fights, at risk of ending the day with fingers swollen and cracked by chilblains. Not even the warm urine baths with which their mothers treat their chilblains are enough to calm the urge. The game is worth the pain, and the snow doesn't last long here once the sun comes out again.

At Sidi M'Cid, at the foot of the cliff, the swimming pool fed by the waterfall always stays usable. Alfred continues his training in water that never drops below twenty-two degrees Celsius. But he knows that his life is about to change dramatically. In the offices of the city's swimming club, the Jeunesse Nautique Constantinoise, Gabriel Menut, the sports director, was definite about it: 'You have to leave,

Alfred, go rub shoulders with the best. Your future is now in Metropolitan France.'

Paris – a leap into the unknown. Far from his parents, his sister, his little brothers. And also far from Paule and her great peals of laughter. She has promised to join him there one day. Since getting together with Alfred, she has begun to swim more regularly. She doesn't dream of being a champion but could well imagine becoming a sports teacher, and why not a swimming teacher? She has already spoken about it to her parents, who have family in Paris. Not a day goes by without her badgering them. For their part, Alfred's parents are preparing for the departure of their little prodigy. When his stepmother, Rose, was told of his decision, she burst into tears. His grandmother, Sarah, took refuge in the kitchen, where she silently made lemon and cinnamon pastries. His father, David, broke into a big smile. Ever since the Christmas Cup, he who had always been so sceptical about Alfred's sporting ambitions has firmly supported him. As for Alfred's little brothers, Prosper and Roger, they prefer to say goodbye by playing silly jokes on him rather than by hugging him.

Alfred is crossing the sea for the first time. From the afterdeck of the *Ville d'Alger*, a magnificent steel steamship built two years earlier in Saint-Nazaire, his hands icy from the cold, he watches the only land he's ever known disappear. He has barely set foot in Paris when he's overwhelmed by a wave of homesickness that is even stronger than his wonderment at discovering the City of Light. Where is the Mediterranean sky hiding? The scent of the orange flowers? Where are his rocky cliffs of Constantine, his suspension bridge, his reputedly impregnable city, known to its Jewish inhabitants as 'Little Jerusalem'? The Arabs call it 'Blad al hawa', which, according to Alfred's father, means the *Aerial City* or the *City of the Ravine*, or even the *City of Passions*, whichever you prefer.

Alfred feels a bit lost in this flat, inorganic universe. Only the Eiffel Tower reminds him of the dizzying metal bridges that span the Rhumel gorge. Yet it's here that his life takes a new turn; here that the sacrifice of moving away is supposed to produce the greatest rewards. Here he is, aged seventeen, exiled, uprooted, feeling a thousand contradictory emotions. Far from his family, the love of his life, yet intoxicated by what he is told will be a radiant future.

Alfred has been awarded a scholarship. He is to be a boarder at the Lycée Janson-de-Sailly, a posh establishment on the Rue de la Pompe, in the 16th arrondissement of Paris. The first time he goes there, he stops in front of the courtyard garden at the main entrance: four squares of perfectly mown grass and in the centre a pool of azure blue water, which he would love to dip his feet in, if it weren't strictly forbidden. Perfectly geometrical and straight, almost too much so, he thinks, having grown up in a tangle of alleyways, dead ends, shady squares and jumbled, crooked houses.

Last year, Viviane Sellier, his French teacher at the Lycée d'Aumale, had read aloud in class what Alexandre Dumas, the author of *The Three Musketeers*, had written about the Jewish quarter of Constantine. Alfred had meticulously copied these lines in his exercise book, because the description seemed accurate to him: 'An inextricable network of alleyways stretching through a maze of incomprehensible buildings; openings that seem to lead to passages that end in nothing, apparent entries without exits, semblances of houses where it is impossible to distinguish the sides or point out the front.' A joyful mess, where Europeans, on the other side of an invisible line that crosses the city, hardly ever venture.

At the Lycée Janson, Alfred enrols in the final year to prepare for the second part of his baccalaureate. In the classroom, in front of pupils standing to attention, the headmaster introduces him as a potential swimming star, just arrived from Algeria. With his thick black hair, bushy eyebrows, dark skin and a torso so muscular that his shirt threatens to split at the slightest movement, Alfred certainly stands out.

'I'm relying on you to ensure that Monsieur Nakache adapts as well as possible to his new life in Paris,' orders

Monsieur Legrand. He then launches into a little impromptu test: 'Who can tell me something about Algeria?'

'A Department of France!' shouts a pupil.

'Since when?'

'1870!'

'Reread your lessons, my boy. This great adventure began in 1830, exactly a century ago.'

Alfred knows this bit of history like the back of his hand. In Constantine you can't take a step without coming across a statue of one of the heroes of the conquest. They're presented as heroes, at any rate. How many streets, squares and avenues bear the names of French soldiers who came to subjugate this corner of the Mediterranean? The Duc de Nemours, the son of King Louis-Philippe, Colonel Lamoricière who led the attack, Generals Caraman and Damrémont – there are statues of them all in the city. They look proud, domineering, sculpted for eternity. At the base of the huge statue of Lamoricière, his sabre drawn, is a soldier blowing a bugle call. Alfred knows that the truth is less glorious. One day when his class was on a school trip to the heights of Constantine, his history teacher, Madame Cherki, had whispered to him: 'The capture of the city in October 1837 was brutal. A massacre, a bloodbath.'

'How do you mean?'

'Never forget that, under threat of the French soldiers, the locals hurriedly tied ropes to the ramparts to escape down the cliff face into the Rhumel gorge. The descent became sheer hell. One by one, the ropes broke, and the men crashed down onto the rocks in their hundreds.'

No, Alfred hasn't forgotten. His attachment to Constantine goes beyond the communities that make up this cosmopolitan city. Muslims, Jews, Catholics, all are first and foremost citizens of Constantine. In the gardens of the school, Alfred tries to adopt the best possible attitude: relaxed, smiling, quick to respond, with a few shafts of humour, like his brothers. A short pupil, wearing round spectacles that make him look bookish, soon takes a liking to him. His name is Émile, he lives locally and is the son and grandson of bakers. His grandfather started his trade in the most beautiful palace of the age, the Hotel Frascati in Le Havre.

'That's where the fashion for sea-bathing began,' says Émile, as they walk along the paths. 'On the main beach of Le Havre or at the foot of the cliffs of Étretat, women were taken to the water's edge in horse-drawn bathing machines. After that, strong men carried them in their arms and lowered them into the sea. My grandfather called it "bathing on the edge".'

Émile isn't trying to be smart or show off his knowledge, he just wants to share it. He has a kindly nature and is generous, as Alfred likes people to be. Émile admits to being useless at gymnastics and a poor swimmer, but says he's passionate about sport. Every week his father buys him the sporting journal *Le Miroir des sports* and he religiously cuts out the best articles, filing them by discipline.

'Football and boxing are what I like best,' he enthuses. 'Occasionally my father takes me to see football matches when CAP Charenton are playing at the stadium in Colombes or to the Salle Wagram to watch Marcel Thil boxing. He's my absolute idol. "The man with the iron fists".'

'I'd really like to see Henry Armstrong in the ring! I adore the Yanks. Do you know anything about swimming?'

'Not much. Apart from Jean Taris, of course, the first Frenchman to swim the 100 metres freestyle in under a minute.'

'Yes, he's the greatest. Eight world records in two years. He'll bring home a gold medal for us at the Olympic Games.'

'He almost did before, didn't he?'

'Last year at the Los Angeles Olympics, he missed out by a hair's breadth. In the 400 metres freestyle, there was only a tenth of a second between him and that handsome American Buster Crabbe, the one the ladies love.'[12]

'Do you dream of going to the Olympics?'

'Too soon to think about it. Maybe one day.'

'I'd put money on it!' cries Émile passionately. 'If that happens, you'll be the only gold medallist I've ever shaken hands with.'

In his eyes, Alfred sees more than kindness: he sees

admiration. He's happy about that. Émile will become his friend in all circumstances, as true friends are. But there are others at the school whose eyes don't light up in the same way when they meet him, who give him a black look instead. He's Jewish, and he's well aware that they're not too fond of Jews here. More than once, he's on the receiving end of their sarcastic comments, their insinuations and insults. These people are not the majority, but their attacks hurt. One of them apes his gait, waddling like a duck with his feet turned out, another taunts him by making fun of his name, calling him Alfred Cache-Cache [hide and seek] – who wants to play hide and seek with Alfred? – and then continues on his way with a great roar of laughter.

Mostly it's just *Jew, Jew*, whispered as he passes along a corridor packed with pupils, so he can't identify whose mouth it's coming from. It sounds like a hissing snake, sly but also ferocious. His father had warned him about the growing hatred of Jews in Europe. *Keep your head up and keep smiling, my boy*, that was the only piece of advice he'd given him. So he smiles, pretends to be indifferent or surprised and amused, suppressing the little twinges of sadness he feels. Often he surprises himself by sticking out his tongue like a street urchin, just like he used to do when his brothers annoyed him. He sticks his tongue out and makes big round eyes. *Faced with a bunch of idiots, you might as well act the clown.*

Sometimes, Émile accompanies him to training sessions at the pool of the Paris Swimming Club, always with a copy of the *Miroir des sports* under his arm. He seems delighted by the spectacle of the swimmers. He gets to admire the great Jean Taris, the undisputed king of the crawl, who is becoming more of a godfather to Alfred than a role model. When Alfred swims past Émile, he notices his friend's head going back and forth like a windscreen-wiper: one eye on Alfred's lane, the other on the football column of his magazines. Alfred envies him for being like this, cool as a cucumber, honing his football knowledge, while he, Alfred, spends hours killing himself in the water.

He also feels that not everyone at the club is his friend either. Jacques Cartonnet, in particular, the leading breaststroke swimmer. Everyone in the team calls him 'Carton'. He's as long and slender as Alfred is stocky and muscular. A supple and elegant swimmer, he never even seems to be pulling with his arms. When Carton gets out of the water, he's barely out of breath. He nonchalantly dons a bathrobe, combs his hair while holding a little mirror in one hand, then starts conversations in that slightly snooty accent of his that makes everyone else feel like a country bumpkin. According to several articles Alfred has read, Carton comes from an upper middle class Parisian family, and he clearly doesn't miss an opportunity to remind people of that fact. Just like he never forgets to look Alfred up and down and ask him, in front of others: 'Where is it you come from, again? I didn't know people learned to swim out in the sticks . . .'

Poor idiot. Alfred doesn't stick out his tongue, even though he's dying to, and contents himself with following his father's advice and responding with his most beautiful smile. But he knew at first sight that one day this man might cause him problems.

* * *

Alongside his training sessions, Alfred starts classes that will lead to a qualification as a gym teacher. A little theory, a lot of practice and the prospect of eventually earning his living. Apart from the medals, his victories don't bring in a single penny. And Cartonnet's continual goading is starting to get to him. How many times does he suffer from stomach cramps? Often, while he's walking, he repeats to himself the words of resignation that he will address to the head of French swimming: *I made a mistake, please accept my apologies, the pressure is too great.* But the thing is, two days in the dry, away from the pool, and he's itching for the sensation of gliding through the water. It's physical. He's like a withered plant, all shrivelled up, waiting for water to restore its strength, vitality and colour. He's intoxicated by speed, in crawl and more recently in butterfly, the event reserved for the strong and brawny who slice through the water, a feeling he senses could become addictive. Nakache may not have the elegance of Carton, the great stylist, the artist of the pool, he may be no more than ploughman in the pool himself, but the more he swims, the faster he goes, swallowing the water, hitting the waves, picking off of his opponents one by one to crash into the final wall. *Who knows, Cartonnet? One day, the hick from Constantine, the little Jew from the coast of Algeria, will leave you behind with your upper-class arrogance . . .*

Paule, Spring 1934

Could this be the best day of his life? Paule has made her decision. She has persuaded her parents to let her go to Paris to live with her great-uncle Mickaël, an orthopaedic surgeon at the Hôtel-Dieu hospital on the Ile de la Cité. Everyone on the other side of the Mediterranean is very proud of his success. Mickaël and his wife Maud live on the Rue du Faubourg-Saint-Antoine, near the Bastille, in a large apartment. Paule will have her own spacious room there. Like Alfred, she will study in Paris and become a PE teacher. On a pretty postcard with a donkey in the foreground and the deep valleys and the Sidi M'Cid swimming pool visible in the distance, she wrote:

Dear Alfred, it's been decided, I'm coming to join you. Mum and Dad believe in us. Their admiration for you is equalled only by mine – infinite. I want to be by your side, laugh with you and support you. I want to be your wife forever.

A few months later, outside the École normale supérieure

d'éducation physique, the training college for physical education teachers, they meet again at last. They embrace, two young people who are not quite adults yet but who are planning their future together, certain of their destiny. They make a habit of going for a walk in the gardens of the Trocadéro or the Parc Monceau after class. He talks to her about swimming, the hopes people pin on him, his upcoming competitions and the enormous pleasure he gets from gliding through the water, from being fast, but also about the increasingly frequent gnawing doubts that make him want to give it all up.

Alfred misses Constantine, and so does Paule. He's worried about Constantine. On 5 August 1934, their families were scared: the Jewish quarter was besieged by rioting Muslims. Twenty-five deaths in the Jewish community, including six women and four children, and more than two hundred shops ransacked. In the Rue Abdallah-Bey and the Rue des Zouaves, two families were stabbed to death in their homes. The riots spread to Aïn Beïda, Sétif and several villages to the east. His stepmother Rose tells him in a distraught letter that it all started because a tipsy Jew was said to have insulted a Muslim at prayer. 'And to think,' she writes, 'that in Kar Chara we hear both the cathedral bells and the calls of the muezzins from their white minarets! What's happening to us? I'm afraid, my children, that our district is aptly named: on the brink of the abyss . . .'

For all the Jews of Constantine, 5 August does indeed mark a turning point. A part of their world collapses with this first pogrom on Algerian soil. Collective violence, previously unimaginable, that could break out again at any time. For several weeks, Alfred had been hearing about new tensions between Jews and Muslims. After the shockwave of the financial crash of 1929, the Arab farmers and small shopkeepers had become impoverished and there was growing resentment towards the wholesalers, most of whom were Jews, who were thought to be getting away unscathed. The French administration had apparently also decided to stop issuing hunting permits to Muslims, allowing the Jews to freely arm themselves with rifles.

Some people, such as Dr Bendjelloul, the charismatic Muslim tribune of Constantine, believe they are experiencing the reversal of the centuries-old order of *dhimmi* status,[13] and there is a feeling that Jews now rank above Muslims and are taking advantage of this status to show contempt for Islam. Add to that the outbursts of Henri Lautier, a pathological antisemite who pits Muslims against Jews and covers the walls of the city with slogans like 'Constantine = Youpinville' (a derogatory name that means something like 'Jewsville'), and everything comes together at the first skirmish to shatter the *Andalusian* harmony so cherished by Rose and the vast majority of Constantine's citizens.[14]

Sitting on a bench overlooking the rotunda at the entrance of the park, Alfred allows himself to be overwhelmed by a strange feeling, a mixture of sadness and despondency. His stomach is still in painful knots. And for the first time since leaving Algeria, tears run down his face. He hates crying, especially in front of others. But this time, he doesn't just weep, he dissolves into tears. A torrent of salt water, a dam giving way, an uncontrollable flood. He hiccups like a child, surrounded by a flock of cooing pigeons that take no notice of him. Where is this uninterrupted flow coming from? He feels wretched. His cousin used to call him a wimp. He was right. Paule comes up to him, takes out a handkerchief and gently wipes his cheeks. Better than anyone, she understands his feeling of being uprooted. Only long-term exiles who flee their country to save their skin or who, like him, leave to pursue a great dream, know this state of indecision and solitude that leaves them adrift without a compass.

Softly, she whispers in his ear: 'Alfred, how many boys and girls do you think dream of achieving success in an activity they excel in? They all do! And as they lie in bed at night, they curse themselves for not being talented enough or, if they have talent, for not having the energy, the persistence, the perseverance to go all the way. You have this opportunity, Alfred, this great opportunity, and all the people applauding you at the side of the pool will experience through you what they would have loved to achieve themselves. No one more than me.'

'You're very kind, Paule.'

'I really believe it. You know the parable of the talents: What have you done with your talent?'

'Never heard of it.'

'I'll bring you the text tomorrow. It's a Christian parable a friend told me about. It means that all God's children must make their talents bear fruit, for themselves and, above all, for others.' Then with a sudden burst of laughter she adds: 'My only talent is having met you!'

The king of the water

On this Sunday afternoon, they are walking along the shady avenues of the Luxembourg Gardens, stopping in front of the greenhouses full of fruit trees that remind them of the orange trees in Constantine. They continue towards the pond, where they admire the model ships that the local children control, after a fashion, with long sticks. The cinema they are heading to, the Studio des Ursulines, is nearby. The film they have chosen to see is neither a beautiful love story nor the hilarious *Duck Soup* by the Marx Brothers, which has recently been released in France, but a short documentary about Jean Taris, Alfred's idol and fellow swimmer. Jean Vigo,[15] a young film-maker popular in Paris, was interested in the 'King of the Water', as he calls Taris. This film was largely shot underwater in the pool of the Automobile Club – a first in the world of cinema – and it's the talk of the city's swimming pools. Paule and Alfred, cuddled up together in the cinema, watch nine minutes of superb images that are also filled with humour.

Vigo's screenplay seems to vacillate between parody, admiration and swimming lesson. Up on the screen, the swimming-pool referee is equipped with a gigantic, intentionally ridiculous-looking megaphone, which makes Alfred smile. 'Allo, allo!' yells the man in the suit. On the starting block is Jean, the holder of twenty-three French national records at every distance from 100 to 1,500 metres, the world-record holder at 800 metres . . . 'Ready, get set . . .?' Then there's the crack of the starting pistol, and Jean swimming length after length at terrific speed through water bubbling with silvery reflections. Then Vigo mischievously makes the great champion leave the pool in reverse, as if he's rewinding his film. There is Jean again, back on the starting block, facing the camera and offering the novice spectators a swimming lesson.

With amused authority, Taris describes the profile of the typical swimmer: 'Water is his domain, as it is for fish. Of course he has to learn a few movements, but all he has to do is enter the water. You don't learn to swim in a room. Personally, I swim crawl, because it's suitable for both long-distance and speed swimming.' Alfred savours his hero's words. Humble, precise, sometimes tinged with self-mockery. For the boy from Constantine, Paris rhymes with

Taris, he repeats the line from the newspapers. He follows Taris's advice to the letter. *At the start, strong push with the legs, relaxed arms, be almost flat when you make contact with the water . . .*

In the semi-darkness of the Studio des Ursulines, Paule is still curled up in Alfred's arms when 'The End' appears on the screen in large letters. Neither of them wants to get up.

'Suppose we treat ourselves to a second showing,' she says.

★ ★ ★

At every training session, Alfred applies and retains what he's told, until he's on the cusp of catching up with his hero. At the French championships held in September 1934 at the Piscine des Tourelles in Paris, he finishes second in the crawl, just behind Taris, in 1 minute 2.4 seconds. This performance earns him his first selection for the French team and headlines in the press. 'The winner, Taris,' it says in the sports paper *L'Auto*, 'on the point of being devoured by the lion Nakache, managed to avoid the blow from the dangerous animal's paw and finally overcame him.' The following year in Bordeaux, on 21 July 1935, Alfred dethrones him and feels almost ashamed of doing so. After this title win, profiles of the young North-African champion crop up all over the papers, half admiring, half intrigued. Is it his foreign-looking face that arouses their curiosity? The way he now sticks out his tongue at the end of every race – in jest and not in provocation, as some journalists write? Or is it rather the inelegant way in which he swims – like a removal man, ugly but ultra-fast – that surprises and repels the finer minds of swimming? Maybe a bit of all three.

In the papers, he's portrayed as the brilliant oaf of freestyle – at least there's that. 'The champion with the invincible fighting spirit,' writes Émile-Georges Drigny, the former swimmer who organized the swimming events at the Paris Olympics in 1924. In *Le Miroir des sports*, this leading light of the sport gently carves him up: 'Nakache is not the product of perfect adaptation, of a true mechanization adapted to the best style, as his swimming is far from achieving perfection: essentially his value lies in his fighting spirit.' And for those who might not have properly understood, he adds: 'Without assigning or bringing to his training too much in the way of method or perseverance, Nakache relies mainly on his moral qualities. Beneath a down-to-earth and sometimes nonchalant attitude, the North-African swimmer hides a will that is remarkable in every way.' Paule cuts out everything that's written about him, enthusing over the glowing headlines and putting the slightest critical comment into perspective. 'Do it and let them talk' is his guiding principle, as well as his shield. Gradually Alfred climbs the ladder of success and fame, winning more and more trophies and medals. His coach, Georges Hermant, doesn't try to correct his technique. He has understood that Alfred's real trump card is his power. That, and the rage that comes over him during his races.

At the same time, a new stroke is emerging: butterfly. The technique involves pushing from the hips to raise the shoulders as high as possible and stretching the arms to their maximum width, then coming down again with an undulating motion through the whole body, sweeping back great volumes of water. A series of leaps in the water, in a way. Only the most physical of swimmers can handle this stroke – most collapse at the end of a length, literally breathless.

'This stroke is going to become the most spectacular and popular in the world,' Alfred's coach keeps telling him. 'It was made for you.'

April 1935 – The temptation
of Tel Aviv

What is he doing here in Tel Aviv, in the sunshine of Palestine, among thousands of Jewish athletes ready to compete in most of the disciplines of the Olympic Games? For Alfred, the 1936 summer Olympics in Berlin, which were awarded to Germany in 1931, two years before Hitler rose to power, are still a distant and uncertain horizon. But this sporting event in Palestine, the Maccabiah, to which he was invited by the Zionist movement, is very important to him. It's the second ever to be held, after the first in 1932. These games are as much about bringing together Jewish athletes from all over the world as they are about breaking records –1,350 athletes from 28 countries. The British High Commissioner in Palestine, Sir Arthur Wauchope, has given his consent, on the condition that Arab athletes and competitors from the British Mandate may also participate.

For Alfred, it's a trial run, a dip into the light and perfumes that reawaken the scents of Constantine within him, and also being part of the dream of a future Jewish land in the Middle East. A demonstration of strength as well. In Paris, Alfred has often talked about it with members of the Maccabi, the Jewish sports clubs that recruit from the middle classes. The time has come to break with the antisemitic cliché of the 'poor, puny and scared Jew' through a 'culture of the body and physical effort', and not only a 'culture of study'.

Alfred remembers the strange expression 'muscular Judaism' that one of his uncles in Constantine had used one day to persuade him to toughen up. At the time, he hadn't really understood what it meant. Later he had been made to read the writings of Max Nordau, the author of this doctrine based on the 'muscular Christianity' of the Protestants: 'We need to return to being men with brawny chests, athletic bodies and a bold gaze, and we must raise agile, supple, muscular young people who will grow up to resemble our ancestors, the Hasmoneans, the Maccabees and Bar Kokhba. They must be fit to take part in the heroic battles of all nations.'

It's fair to say that Alfred, with his body hewn from rock, has taken this lesson to heart. That day in the pool in Tel Aviv, to the cheers of spectators from all over the world, he wins a beautiful silver medal in the freestyle, a reward for this return trip full of promises.

Auschwitz – In the attics

The emaciated bodies approaching the infirmary no longer look human. Their eye sockets are enlarged, giving them a fixed, expressionless gaze that tells a story of emptiness rather than drama.

Professor Robert Waitz is wonderfully devoted and compassionate. The dispensary he's in charge of fills six blocks, from 14 to 20, but most of the equipment is kept in block 18. Alfred is proud to be one of his assistants. Together they heal wounds, lance abscesses and boils and soothe the unbearable itching caused by skin diseases. They have also set up a network for stealing bread and beetroot jam, which they distribute discreetly in the blocks. Sometimes they try to comfort these broken souls with a kind word or a joke.

Professor Waitz soon asks Alfred to call him by his first name. At the age of forty-four, he is an imposing figure with his broad forehead, slicked-back hair and big white coat. He asks Alfred countless questions about his background and the fear of water that he managed to overcome. Little by little, when the treatment room empties, he also opens up about the secret side of his career.

'After the surrender, all the researchers and doctors at the University of Strasbourg withdrew to Clermont-Ferrand, in the *zone libre*. It's a beautiful region, with snow-covered volcanic domes and frozen lakes in winter that make you think of the vast open spaces of Canada. That's where we started to get organized.'

'In a network?'

Waitz comes closer and whispers. 'First, the *francs-tireurs* of Auvergne, then the Unified Resistance Movements. I became their number two. After the Gestapo entered the southern zone, we increased the sabotage. And then I fell into a trap. On the morning of 3 July 43 . . .'

'And when did you get here?'

'On 10 October, convoy 60 from Bobigny.'

Robert explains that, on the Nazis' orders, he set up a laboratory for medical analysis and that he was not entrusted with the dispensary until later. 'You know the rules here, Alfred,' he says. 'The SS show no mercy towards the most seriously ill who are no use for anything. We have to try to hide them, shield them from the roll-call for as long as possible to save them from being killed.'

'How?'

He looks up towards the ceiling, smiling fixedly at a narrow groove on the right: 'The attics.'

Alfred doesn't believe it. He can't believe it. It's a crazy risk for Robert to take. If he's caught in the act or betrayed, the SS will execute him, despite his being a luminary of medicine. Yet several times, Alfred will help him to hoist men up into this survival space that is pitch black and so cramped you can only crawl there on all fours. Time for Robert to try to help them recover. Or, failing that, at least to offer them a less brutal death.

December 1935

Émile joins his friend Alfred at the Coupole on the Boulevard du Montparnasse, one of their favourite restaurants. He's brought the book that Jacques Cartonnet has just written, which is simply entitled *Nages* (Swimming Strokes).[16] The thirty-two illustrations are magnificent: the perfect movements for each stroke are dissected in detail, as are the dives performed by a superb female swimmer with slicked-back blond hair. *Swallow dive from a standing start, forward kip, twist, forward somersault, tuck or pike* . . . The photographs look extremely graceful.

'D'you reckon he's found his Marlene Dietrich?' jokes Alfred as he leafs through the book. 'There's something of a blue angel and a blonde Venus about this pretty creature, don't you think?'

'You're right, he's picked a good model. Apart from that, I've only read the preface. A "letter to an unknown friend". I'm not sure I understood everything . . .'

Alfred snatches the book from his hands and reads the last lines as he sips his anisette.

The struggle of the body against the water awakens dormant truths, without which courage resolves into formulae. It overcomes the lassitude of existence and the deformations of a physical perfection in which the fullness of the moral being is revealed. And if it encourages men to meet on riverbanks or around water imprisoned by paved rectangles, it is because there is room today for a heroic life.

'The moral being, the heroic life,' sighs Alfred. 'But what does this man understand by truth?'

Paris, March 1936

Georges Hermant has finally published the list of swimmers selected for the Olympic Games in Berlin. He let them know them the previous evening, one by one, in his little office just off the swimming pool at the Racing Club de France. Apart from swimming techniques, he's also keen on tales of adventure and exploration, and the timber walls of his sanctum are covered with shelves overflowing with books and magazines.

Hermant is an enthusiast. Above all, he's a well-respected man, who always finds the right words to encourage, congratulate or console someone. He gets up, walks round his desk, places a chair next to Alfred's and takes a drag of his cigarette.

'What a long way you've come, my boy, what a long way! In three months, it'll be your first Olympics. You really deserve to be selected for the team. They'll be cheering down in Constantine.'

Alfred feels his cheeks reddening, as always happens when he's overcome with emotion. That's how it was back in his schooldays, when he was called up to the blackboard. And it never fails to happen even now, when he's asked to speak in public – crimson face, words getting mixed up, a disaster.

'I'll try to live up to expectations. Thank you. Thanks for everything.'

Those are the only words he can find, the great Nakache. Hermant smiles and looks towards the door.

'Off you go. And get to work, Alfred. If you want to call your parents, you can use my phone.'

Before meeting up with Paule at her uncle's, Alfred went to the florist's to buy a bunch of white roses. Twenty-two, as if he were celebrating her birthday that day. He also stopped at the wine merchant's on the Rue de Seine, where the resident champagne lover recommended a Henriot rosé. With his hands full, Alfred rang the doorbell of the flat. Paule opened the door. He stuck out his tongue, rolling his black eyes like billiard balls. The return of the clown. She stammered, her eyes wide: 'The Olympics?'

'Yes, the Olympics, my love. In Berlin!'

Berlin . . . They're so happy that they'd rather not think about all that. The capital of the Third Reich, the Nazi parades, Hitler's rages. The dreadful Nuremberg Race Laws, approved in September 1935, that make German

Jews foreigners in their own country. They know that Jewish teachers there have been dismissed. It's in all the papers. Since April 1933, Jews have also been excluded from sports clubs and from being selected for the national teams. Like everyone else, Alfred and Paule have read the calls for a boycott on the posters in the streets of Paris: 'No athletes to Berlin!' Posters reminding people that two German sportsmen have been sentenced to life imprisonment for daring to say that sporting freedom no longer existed in their country. 'Going to Berlin,' write the signatories to the appeal, 'is legitimizing Hitler's atrocities. Not going to Berlin is striving for the brotherhood of nations and races. Not going to Berlin is reinforcing peace!' In the evenings, Alfred and Paule are often overcome with anxiety but, like most of the Jews they know, they want to remain optimistic.

France has its own reasons for abandoning the idea of boycotting the Olympics. The Winter Olympics in Garmisch-Partenkirchen in February went off well, and the French team returned delighted. Pierre de Coubertin, the co-founder of the modern Olympics, assured everyone that Hitler respected the Olympic spirit. As for the attempt by French and Spanish workers' movements to organize an antifascist 'People's Olympiad' in Barcelona, that failed in the end at the news of a military uprising throughout the whole of Spain. The foreign athletes and visitors, including the seventy members of the Yiddischer Arbeiter Sport Klub

(YASK) from Paris, were repatriated by special boat as a matter of urgency.

So Alfred reckons it's best to forget the appalling words of this mere corporal turned dictator, with his puppet-like rigidity and his crazy eyes. He'll have to act as though Hitler didn't exist. Repeat to himself that it's only sport – the most beautiful and splendid of sports events. And above all, tell himself that, contrary to all expectations, a little Jew from Constantine made the team ahead of Cartonnet.

Berlin, August 1936

It's the opening day of the Berlin games, 1 August 1936. In the huge Olympic stadium, wearing blue jackets and white trousers, they don't do the Nazi salute with their arms stretched out horizontally, but the Olympic salute, which looks similar. Is Hitler still in the stands? They can't be sure, from where they're standing. If he's watching them, the Führer must be revelling in this general submission. But in their minds, they are delighted to be pulling a fast one on him.

Since arriving in Berlin, the French athletes have been awestruck by the excess surrounding them. There's the stadium that seats 100,000, of course, but also the ultra-modern Olympic village that houses the 4,400 sportsmen and 360 sportswomen who have been selected to take part in these Games. The French press is full of admiration for the millimetre precision of the organization of these eleventh Olympic Games. There are 2,800 journalists on site. For the first time in history, a direct radio broadcast is being made available to 150 foreign radio stations with 300 million listeners around the world. Newspaper columnists are bowled over by the architectural splendour of the capital of the Third Reich: the broad avenues bedecked with swastikas; the buildings that look swollen with pride, like the gigantic tower housing the bronze Olympic bell; the monumental sculptures. Alfred, however, finds all this pretentious pomp horribly sad. Above all, the city feels tense, with its motorized patrols and its parades of helmeted, white-gloved soldiers pounding the streets in goose step. A sinister spectacle that leaves little room for peace, and less still for fun.

In fact, for Alfred, it's really no fun at all. Feeling under the weather, suffering from a bloated stomach, on 8 August he has to withdraw from the quarter finals of the 100 metres freestyle, an event in which he has every chance. With his teammates Christian Talli, René Cavalero and Jean Taris, his idol, everything now rests on the relay races. On 12 August, it's the 4 x 200 metres freestyle – the last chance to bring back a medal. But in the vast Olympic swimming pool, in front of thousands of spectators, things don't go their way. The other three aren't in top form either. They miss the podium by a fraction of a second.

Fourth, the worst possible place, behind the Americans, the Japanese and the Hungarians. The only satisfaction: in a climate of intensified rivalry, they beat the Germans.[17]

★ ★ ★

Alfred spends a good part of the flight back to Le Bourget sitting next to the boxer Roger Michelot. The light-heavyweight is a gold medallist, just like his fellow competitor Jean Despeaux in the middleweight category. Two gold medals for the noble art, out of the seven won by the French! For a boxing fan like Alfred, this offers some compensation for the poor showing of the swimmers, with no medals.

Michelot also beat a German in the final, Richard Vogt – a splendid fight that Alfred and Taris attended together. It's an experience they won't be forgetting any time soon. Both are delighted by it.

'Apparently Hitler was furious!' laughs Michelot.

'Did you see? Vogt climbed into the ring with the Olympic belt round his waist.'

'Too sure of himself, that fellow. He beat me four years ago in the semi-finals in Los Angeles. He's a head taller than me, with muscles like steel. He thought it was a foregone conclusion.'

'I know some cocky swimmers like that too. What you did to him, my God! You were moving better than him, we could see that straight away.'

Michelot hands Alfred the latest edition of *L'Auto*, hot off the press. 'Read that,' he says.

Third round. The Germans are frantically applauding their favourite. Vogt doesn't allow himself to be

out-manoeuvred and catches up a bit on points. A
terrific exchange of blows, in which Michelot looks more
skilful and Vogt more fiery. A magnificent right from
the Frenchman finds its mark, the German's jaw, and
the bell goes. Michelot is the winner!

'You see, Roger, in the water, I'm more the aggressive
type. I'll have to work on my style,' says Alfred.

With a knowing look, Michelot pats him on the shoulder.
He's clutching his medal in his hand. As Alfred goes back
to his seat, he sees Michelot smiling at the sea of clouds, his
face glued to the window.

December 1936 – The hour
of the duel

At training, Jacques Cartonnet looks Alfred up and down with more than his usual arrogance. He has decided to no longer speak to the man who was selected for the Berlin Olympics. He doesn't talk to Alfred anymore, but he doesn't take his eyes off him. A sneaky, sideways look. *If he'd just decide to ignore me completely, things would be easier!* What has Cartonnet got against Nakache? Evidently, he can't get over the snub of not being chosen for Berlin. And then there's his fear of being deposed once and for all by some foreigner who swims clumsily – he, the artist of the pool, flattering profiles of whom still appear in the newspapers. All those articles glorifying him are quite something, practically declarations of love: 'Jacques Cartonnet. Height: 1 metre 79. Beautifully proportioned: 79 kilos. The power of his rib cage doesn't preclude an elegance of line.' Or even better: 'Pale eyes, an almost innocent smile, a slow, gentle voice. The torso of a colossus and a profusion of muscles. The head of a boy on the body of a cyclops.' *Maybe he simply can't stand Jews*, muses Alfred. Cartonnet is wary of venturing into this territory, but contempt oozes out of him like beads of sweat.

Alfred knows he mustn't let himself be consumed by this elusive being. He decides to provoke him, quite fairly, by challenging him in breaststroke, the discipline at which Carton has excelled for years. Alfred even announces this duel to the press. After all, attack is the best form of defence. He suggests a 100-metre race. A sprint. To those who are surprised, he responds in *Paris-Soir*, the daily newspaper: 'They called me insolent when I announced that I wished to challenge Jacques Cartonnet to a 100-metre breaststroke race. Of course I know that this is a perilous adventure, but I like adventures. I like this one even more than others because of the risks involved.' When Carton, who is no longer speaking to Alfred, reads the paper, he hits the roof. You'd think he'd forgotten all his good education. In the changing rooms, livid with rage, he shouts at Alfred, getting right up in his face: 'Are you trying to act smart? Tomorrow you'll be the disgrace of French swimming. You won't even have the nerve to open a newspaper.'

Alfred listens to him without saying a word. *Think of your father, Alfred, ignore the insults*. On the day of the race, in the magnificent Neptuna swimming pool on the Boulevard de Bonne-Nouvelle, he knows that everyone is waiting for him. The Nakache–Cartonnet duel makes the front pages of the sporting press. The headlines aren't quite the size of those used for boxing matches, but still. They tell him there are hundreds of fans on the terraces, radio reporters, members of parliament, ministers – all the bigwigs. But the only thing that matters to him is Paule's confident gaze. He wants to win for her. He's going to win for her.

He makes a perfect start, putting all his explosive power into it. In the next lane, Cartonnet stretches out but is half a second behind him, maybe as much as a second. He won't be able to draw level. It's Alfred's day, his race, the response to Cartonnet's arrogance. His lungs are full to bursting. He's aware of the noise of the crowd urging him on, encouraging him. A wave of shouts and applause bursting like bubbles in his ears. Is it good for him? He feels that the crowd is on his side – on the side of the challenger, the side of the strange swimmer. He gives his all over the last few metres. The pool has become one enormous sound box. He can't distinguish anything in the roar of noise. *One more stroke, Alfred . . .* He touches the wall, his head pops up out of the water, there's nothing but cheering around him, the crowd is on its feet, all eyes are fixed on him. And Paule's beaming face, suddenly standing out as if captured by the keen eye of a photographer.

'The winner is Nakache, in 1 minute, 12.4 seconds!'

With the French record shattered, Alfred savours this brief moment of eternity. It isn't a question of revenge, just a matter of setting the record straight.

October 1937

That morning, in his room at the Janson-de-Sailly school, Alfred receives a parcel that warms his heart. Inside it are the three 78 rpm discs that Cheikh Raymond has recorded for Diamophone, a record label in Constantine. A gift from the artist that had been kept a secret. The records are accompanied by a little handwritten note: 'Dear Alfred, my hands glide over the strings of my instruments like you glide in your swimming lanes. Keep on delighting the Parisians. Your friend at last "engraved" on a disc.'

On hearing the first notes of the oud and the violin, Alfred is back in the flower-covered, scented courtyard of the Funduq Ben-Azéim. Raymond's voice envelops him and takes him back to the city of his childhood, all the while making the sense of loss and distance a little more painful. He misses being teased by his brothers, he misses his grandmother's rich, aromatic cooking and picnics in the sun. After this, not a day goes by without one of Cheikh Raymond's songs running through his head.

Paris, December 1937

At the Piscine des Tourelles, a monumental building erected on the Avenue Gambetta for the 1924 Olympic Games, Jean Taris is already ensconced in the luxurious bar, panelled in pale wood, that overlooks the pool, with a book in his hand, when Alfred turns up at last, smiling broadly. It's now several months since Taris called an end to his career. Enough time to write a small memoir, *La Joie de l'eau* (The Joy of Water),[18] which he wants to give his protégé.

'Perhaps we should have chosen a different place to meet,' Taris says jauntily.

'Why?' mumbles Alfred.

'What! Have you forgotten? It was the ham in their blasted sandwiches that ruined our chances at the Berlin Olympics. The whole team had eaten them and were clutching their stomachs for days. What are you drinking, my boy?'

'The same as you, a glass of red,' replies Alfred who,

despite Jean's repeated invitations, had never managed to address him using the more familiar *tu* rather than the more formal *vous*.

'Here, this is for you,' continues Taris, handing him a copy of his book. 'Jacques Cartonnet won't be the only one to fill the bookshops any more . . .'

'He'll take it very badly,' says Alfred mockingly.

'You won't learn much about technique, but I talk a bit more about myself. If that can persuade a few people to emulate me . . .'

There's no sign of a difference in rank in the way the two men look at one another. There is only the friendly expression of complicity that links two swimmers who know the true price of victory.

'The press are sorry you've gone, Jean.'

'I know, I know, but you have to follow your instinct. I'm not leaving the sport because I don't like it any more, but because I don't want to risk not liking it any more one day.'

'What do you mean?'

'There's nothing sadder than the old champion who gets beaten by everybody because he's not what he used to be, because he doesn't want to give up. He's a bit like those old ladies who still go on simpering when their time is past,' he continues teasingly. 'Come on, let's drink to the joy of the water! And to your future records!'

Alfred quickly leafs through the book, which is peppered

with photos of the champion breaking down the ideal movements of the crawl. He skims through a few lines of the first chapter. '*If only all those who claim that I'm exceptional could have seen me a few years ago. I was a puny teenager, thin and scraggly, narrow-shouldered, weedy-looking . . .*'

'You didn't think you were made for swimming?' says Alfred, looking up in astonishment.

'I was as unlikely to become an athlete as that weightlifter Rigoulot[19] is to be a butterfly hunter. I'm going to make a confession: at secondary school, I was so sickly and weedy they called me the stick insect.'

'People made fun of me because I was afraid of the water.'

'No risk of that, in my case. I was passionate about it. When I was little, I could stay in the water for hours. To begin with, I wanted to play rugby. Obviously, all the skinny kids want to go in for violent sports! My parents took us to see a match and, crash, a player broke his leg right in front of us. My mother's reaction: "That's it, you won't be taking up rugby."'

Alfred realizes that he's never dared to ask his idol personal questions before.

'What about competing, did something trigger that?'

'It certainly wasn't the manager of my first club. When he saw me swim, he said: "Him? No point encouraging him. He'll never be any good." No, my boy, the man who sparked things off is called Weissmuller, Johnny Weissmuller.[20] The first time I saw him was in '24, in the Pages pool at Versailles. The American team had chosen my local pool to prepare for the Olympics. I was fifteen, I was stunned by his power, his style and his elegance. A friend and I agreed we'd copy him. That's how it all started . . .'

'My Weissmuller was called Fabien. An ordinary soldier passing through Constantine. When I think back, I tell myself I owe everything to him.'

Taris cuts him short. 'I have to go, Alfred. One day you'll tell me about it. It's crazy that we haven't talked about this before! In the meantime, pay attention to what Hermant tells you. Always follow your coach's advice, OK? You know his motto: flexibility and breathing . . .'

Alfred doesn't have time to thank him for the book before Taris heads towards the stairs. Just before he disappears, he turns round and, with a note of amusement in his voice, he declaims: 'Flexibility and breathing, Alfred! Believe me, you'll go a long way with that!'

★ ★ ★

La Joie de l'eau has become Alfred's bedside book. Even though the book is intended for beginners, he soaks up his master's advice every night before he falls asleep. He reads it in his own way, searching each sentence for the comment that might lead him to correct a fault. He knows he swims using his strength, relying on his muscle power and his fighting spirit. But his technique has its limits – there is a risk of running out of steam, of breaking down or losing the ability to think clearly. Flexibility and breathing, repeats Taris in his book. 'You don't need to have big muscles in order to be a successful swimmer,' he writes. 'On the contrary, you need to have long, flexible muscles, good lungs and a sound heart. Most of all, you need to learn to swim steadily.' Alfred is delighted by this phrase.

'Listen to this, darling. If I want to progress further, I need to learn to swim steadily. If only I'd known!' he jokes.

Paule puts down *La Femme de France*, the Parisian fashion magazine she immerses herself in every week. She loves the beauty advice, the sketches of chic new outfits that are both elegant and practical – *very sporty*, according to the magazine – but also the society gossip and the stories of the supernatural. She snatches the book out of Alfred's hands and points out that in the first paragraph, Taris starts by talking about long distance races – in particular, the Traversée de Paris, an eight-kilometre swim in the swirling waters of the Seine that he has won several times.

'Read this, you idiot,' she says affectionately. '"Personally, I have always won my Traversées de Paris several minutes ahead of my rivals, without getting tired or losing my rhythm, because I swam 'steadily'." That's very different from a 200-metre race, my love!'

'Hermant is always telling me to stretch out and relax. That's how Cartonnet made his reputation.'

'Forget about him, he's nothing.'

Alfred turns the pages and stops at the part about Weissmuller, the man who inspired Taris and who has now found success playing Tarzan on the silver screen. *Tarzan the Ape Man*, *Tarzan and his Mate* and *Tarzan Escapes* – Alfred and Paule have watched that last film three times at the Caméo, the cinema on the Boulevard des Italiens. Like everyone in France, they think of Cheeta as their mascot. And like everyone, or almost everyone, else in the country, Alfred tries to imitate Tarzan's yell, with limited success.

'Listen to this, Weissmuller is talking about healthy living for athletes. And guess what he says.'

'That I should stop making filled doughnuts for you?'

'Not at all! I quote: "It isn't true that a sportsman must give up smoking completely and be wary of certain foods." That's the best news I've had today!'

'What about the next line? "The only essentials are to do nothing to excess and to lead a regular life."'

'One all!' says Alfred, now holding Taris's book wide open so that Paule won't miss a morsel of Weissmuller's guidelines. It's the waking-up and breakfast advice that grabs their attention:

In the morning, there's no staying in bed. As soon as you get up, drink a glass of hot water slowly. Then do a few minutes of exercise with the window wide open. Before breakfast, drink a glass of fruit juice. The best juices are orange, grapefruit or tomato. Breakfast should start with fruit: an apple, a pear or some prunes. Never drink very hot or very cold drinks. And finally, your skin needs to breathe: wear light, loose clothing.

'Breathing, that's all they ever talk about!' says Alfred.

'Let's leave aside the clothing advice,' smiles Paule. 'But as for the glass of hot water when you wake up, no need to make me read more about it, it's a deal!'

'The joy of hot water, that's what Taris should have called his book!' says Alfred with a laugh as he puts down the book.

He's happy with his find. He curls up against Paule's body, and she immediately goes back to reading *La Femme de France*. Under the golden halo of her little opaline lamp, she devours the profile of the *femme solarienne,* in which she doesn't recognize herself at all – 'a woman who understands all aspects of the most difficult questions, for whom Life is a wonderful symphony' – *what crap*, she thinks. Then she stops at a note in the 'In Paris and elsewhere' section, entitled 'The three divine consorts'.

'Do you hear this, Alfred? "They're announcing the fiercest female competitions in Hitler's Reich. In Germany, three women share the intoxication of power: Leni Riefenstahl, Magda Goebbels and Madame Sonnemann-Goering. The first is Hitler's faithful muse, the second is the wife of the minister of propaganda. The third is married to the all-powerful minister of war and of the *Reichswehr*. All three are beautiful, passionate and ambitious. What dark dramas are these jealous women preparing?" Are you still with me, darling? "A smile, a nod or an attractive gesture, the desires of a dictator are enough to determine the fate of the universe. The course of history can still be affected by small things like Cromwell's grain of sand, or Cleopatra's nose . . ." I don't know about Cromwell, but Cleopatra's nose is a bit of an exaggeration, isn't it?'

Alfred responds with a deep sigh. He's already far away, lost in his dreams of becoming a champion.

Flat nose and cunning eyes

For Alfred and Paule, the year 1938 flashes by in a cheerful, carefree Paris. At parties and in dance halls, people do the Lambeth Walk, turning it into a swaying parody of military parades and openly mocking the Führer. Even Maurice Chevalier can't quite believe it: 'Mad gaiety in the capital. Yes, really crazy. It's abnormal, we are having too much fun! We're laughing too loudly! There's a note of hysteria in all this. And we dance! And we have a good time! Let's go, then! This entire period makes you think of the sea when the weather starts to darken and a groundswell batters the ship. The weather is getting stormy . . .'[21] As for Alfred, he's accumulating national and international titles. Five new French championship titles: 100 metres freestyle, 200 metres freestyle, 200 metres breaststroke, 4 x 200 metres relay and 10 x 100 metres relay. 'Overwhelming dominance,' trumpets *Le Miroir des sports*. In the summer, Alfred and Paule are excited by the Football World Cup that is taking place in France, despite their national team being knocked out earlier than hoped, beaten in the quarter finals by the whirling dominance of the Italians, who would go on to win the trophy. Faced with the Squadra Azzurra, the French captain Étienne Mattler, a tough defender known to all as 'the lion of Belfort', was powerless.

Haunted by the rise of antisemitic actions in Germany, in August Alfred refuses to take part in a swimming event in Berlin between the United States and Europe for which he had been selected, opting instead that weekend for the French B team and a meeting between Switzerland and France. 'He prefers Switzerland to the Reich,' writes Jean Brey in *L'Écho des sports*. Georges Hermant, the national coach, doesn't hold it against him. Quite the opposite – he has just found out what happened to Lieutenant Fürstner, the director of the Berlin Olympic village and a distinguished officer whose courtesy and devotion had won over the foreign delegations. Louis Gillet, a journalist and member of the French Academy who had reported from the Games for the monthly magazine *Revue des Deux Mondes*, had revealed the sinister truth in a book.[22] Hermant has marked the page for Alfred: 'Read this, it's quite appalling . . .'

That day, Alfred keeps out of the way in the corridor leading to Hermant's office. Sitting on the narrow bench reserved for visitors waiting to see the boss of French swimming, he slowly reads the passage devoted to Fürstner, fearing the worst:

> He was responsible for maintaining order and harmony in this colourful crowd of athletes that might so easily become sheer bedlam. Unfortunately, he inadvertently let slip that he had a weak point: one of his grandmothers was Jewish. The secret got out; the drop of unclean blood had been discovered. It immediately gave rise to a storm of offensive caricatures, satirical articles and racist barbs.
>
> Every day, von Fürstner found insulting missives in his room. He offered his resignation. Instead of replacing him, they just put him under the nominal command of a colonel, thinking that this precaution would be enough to protect him. His enemies were not fooled. The hunt continued with greater intensity. The officer let nothing show. Until the final day, he could be seen fulfilling all his duties – punctual, affable, ceremonious, correct – and behaving like a man of the world in his difficult role of master of the house.
>
> On the Sunday evening, he said goodbye to his guests, and the next day he was still busy seeing them off and making a final inspection. But on the Tuesday morning, his orderly found him dead.

Alfred's eyes close and his stomach cramps. Images return like ghosts coming to shake him. He thinks back to Fürstner's farewell gesture as he was swallowed up in the car taking him to the airport. A straight look, a kind smile. *Does he already know that his life is over?* Alfred wonders. He pictures the fatal moment when Fürstner takes hold of a weapon, but the screen very quickly becomes blurred – a blank canvas hiding the unthinkable.

For a long time, Alfred continues to be haunted by Gillet's words. *The drop of unclean blood had been discovered. His orderly found him dead.* Then on the night of 9–10 November 1938 comes the shock of *Kristallnacht*, which confirms all their fears. In Berlin, and soon throughout the whole of Germany, shops are destroyed, synagogues burned, thousands of Jews arrested. Rumour has it that this carnage originated with the assassination in Paris of the First Secretary of the German Embassy, Ernst vom Rath, by a seventeen-year-old Polish Jewish refugee, Herschel Grynszpan. A private matter? A political crime? It doesn't matter which. The 'spontaneous popular retaliation' – as the Nazis described the pogrom – hits the Jewish community like a thunderbolt.

★ ★ ★

It's the moment Paule and Alfred have chosen to say yes to one another. Yes to life. Yes to reassure each other. Yes to continue believing in it, despite everything. Their only regret is the fact that their families won't be there, because the trip to Paris would have been too expensive for them. And too dangerous. In Constantine, people are also experiencing the rise of antisemitism and an increase in violent incidents. There is no question of leaving the cousins, nephews and nieces behind alone in a city where the Jewish quarter could become a powder keg at any moment.

They marry in February 1939, at the Synagogue des Tournelles in the Marais district of Paris, in the presence of Uncle Mickaël and his friends. According to tradition, Alfred lifts Paule's veil, revealing her big green eyes, then, under the chuppah, he gives her the wedding ring. Then he in turn receives his ring and, at the end of the ceremony, still following the ritual, breaks a glass with his right foot. It's a way of saying that their marriage will last as long as this glass remains broken, meaning for ever. All evening, surrounded by some twenty guests, they sing and dance to the rhythm of the ma'luf music in the little flat on the Boulevard de Sébastopol that Alfred's coach found for them.

To supplement their monthly income, Paule is now giving gymnastics lessons to the children at the school on the Rue Saint-Martin. She loves teaching. As for Alfred, his career is skyrocketing and the press have given him the nickname Artem. Dimitri Philippoff, a journalist for *L'Auto* who is originally from Moscow, came up with it.

A good swimmer and an excellent water-polo player, he assures Alfred that in Russian 'artem' is the name of an exceptionally fast fish. He can't tell him exactly which fish, but it doesn't matter. Artem has a certain ring to it, and it's a nickname that sticks. In his articles, Philippoff makes fun of Nakache's laid-back attitude. Not realizing that this fundamental characteristic also serves as armour, he writes: 'Despite having lived in Paris for several years, he hasn't felt it necessary to change his behaviour. He isn't afraid of the big city. He hasn't submitted to its rules. What Artem loves and doesn't intend to forget is Constantine. So he walks through the streets of the great, dark centre of Paris, joking, monkeying around and laughing at the sun like a true kid from his country.'

Artem has used some of his savings to buy his first car for 800 francs, a white Simca 5 CV convertible. He waxes enthusiastic in the pages of *Excelsior*, the illustrated daily paper: 'You see me here happy as Larry: married, with a job and the owner of a motor car.'

'So what's still missing?' asks the columnist Roger Lamy.

'To make my happiness complete,' replies Alfred facetiously, 'all I'm waiting for is the right to teach Arabic in schools . . .'

'You have a vocation?' Lamy asks, surprised.

'You mean that it's the only one I have! Like my wife, Paule, I don't know of a job I'd rather have.'

By contrast, Cartonnet is becoming gloomy. Once again, he refuses to compete against Nakache again and withdraws from a 200 metres breaststroke race. His star really is beginning to wane. This time, Alfred is harsh. He is quoted in *Excelsior* again: 'Cartonnet says everywhere that I'm not a breaststroke swimmer worthy of his class. I'm waiting for him to be willing to prove it other than in words, because the only time we've met in a breaststroke race, I beat him.' A stinging headline in a weekly paper reads: 'Have you seen Cartonnet?' Georges Hermant is fuming: 'It's pathetic, Cartonnet's a hopeless character who doesn't like competition and shies away every time he has a serious duty to perform.'

* * *

In the late summer of 1939, probably one of the hottest and most beautiful France has ever seen, dark clouds are gathering. Hitler ramps up his provocations. No one, or hardly anyone, would have imagined he'd go this far. No one, or hardly anyone, was really taking his threats seriously. Even Émile, Alfred's faithful friend, now head of the Bonjean flour mill, wants to be reassuring. Alfred can still remember him saying in December of the previous year: 'Look at Munich, we've really fucked Hitler up.[23] The English government and Édouard Daladier have forced him to accept peace. You only have to see how people cheered for Daladier when he returned to Le Bourget.

And then Ribbentrop, Hitler's Minister of Foreign Affairs, visiting Paris last week, what have you got to say about that? He signed a declaration of Franco-German friendship with great pomp and ceremony. We've won, my friend.'

'No, Émile, we haven't won, we've lost. It's Hitler who's fucked us up. He's annexed yet more territory, so we'll end up declaring war on him. No more carefree life for us, no more paid holidays and no more dancing on the banks of the Marne, we're going to have to fight now. Like in 1914, Émile, it's all kicked off again and we're really in the soup.'

In the press, antisemitic attacks are on the increase. Alfred becomes a favourite target. In *Le Miroir des sports*, someone writes: 'Nakache, with his curly hair, his slightly flat nose and his cunning eyes, his head looking so faun-like that you're surprised to find that he doesn't have pointed ears . . .'

Auschwitz – Fisticuffs

'Did you fall in love straight away?'

'It was love at first sight, for her green eyes.'

'Me too. For her black eyes. But she was far too beautiful for me.'

Behind the barracks, the two champions are taking advantage of a moment's respite, safely out of sight. As the orange streaks of the sunset sky are consumed by darkness, they chat like two pals who no longer have any secrets from one another. Alfred is in better physical shape than his boxer friend, who's exhausted by the excavation work. But as the days continue to pass, his gnawing anxiety increases. He finds it hard to conceal the unfathomable anguish inside him about what fate has in store for Paule and little Annie. Victor reassures him – 'They can't pick on them' – and Alfred pretends to believe him. 'Often, when I pass a woman on one of the paths here, I feel as if I recognize Paule . . .' Those aren't things you imagine, they're promises, Victor assures him. It's been a long time since Victor had a wife. Mireille left him. Mireille Balin, the star of French cinema, the love of his life, who left him alone and in shreds. Alfred senses that Victor needs to talk about it. He listens, encourages him to go on. Talking to bring release.

Victor begins his story with the blessed day when he touched the stars – 24 October 1931, at the Palais des Sports in Paris. Watched by sixteen thousand spectators, at the age of just twenty and to everyone's surprise, he floored the defending world flyweight champion, the American Frankie Genaro, with dazzling footwork followed by a left-right to the chin. Two rounds, a fight lasting barely five minutes, and indescribable jubilation in Tunis, in the Jewish quarter of his childhood. Paris too stares in wide-eyed admiration at this dark-skinned little man with the nickname Younkie. With the insolence of youth, he dethrones the hot favourite and dons the golden mantle of a world champion that is the mark of demi-gods for all eternity.

That's when she appears at a cocktail party where he is the star guest. She's beautiful, refined, a top fashion model for Patou and Coco Chanel, who dreams of going into films. She particularly wants to meet this little phenomenon with the soft eyes and powerful muscles. 'I fall madly in love at first sight. We see each other the same evening, the next day and the day after. We love one another and every second I wonder what's happening to me. How can such an elegant, sought-after woman be besotted with a little Tunisian who's climbed into a boxing ring?'

When she distances herself, Victor puts all his energy into charming her and winning her back. Restaurants, luxury gifts, trips to Deauville in a sports car given to him by Peugeot, casinos – when it comes to keeping hold of Mireille's heart, nothing is too much. 'During this time,' he says, 'I eat dirt. I don't train enough any more, I'm not there any more. I only think of her. In the ring, I let myself get beaten up by my opponents.'

This time, when the mantle of darkness shrouds the sinister line of the brick barracks, Victor continues his journey into the past that reopens all the old wounds. On 31 October 1932, at the Bellevue Casino in Manchester, he again puts his title at risk against the Englishman Jackie Brown.

'Mireille came to watch, dazzling in her Patou jersey and taffeta dress. I'd never seen her looking so beautiful. The photographers were jostling to get near her, with their flashbulbs crackling.'

For the first five rounds, Victor is at the height of his powers, skipping about, brilliantly dodging his opponent's attacks. But in the middle of round six, it all falls apart, his legs grow heavy and his body stops responding.

'I stick to it like a madman, I take a left-right to the stomach, then an incredible series of hooks to the jaw. I fall backwards, get up, stagger, completely dazed. Léon Bellières, my trainer, puts an end to the massacre.'

Victor Perez has lost his title and, while the Parisian press jeers, the look on Mireille's face sends him a cruel image of disappointment. For everybody, Perez has once again become 'the child from the souks'.

However, encouraged by his trainer, the kid from Tunis hasn't given up. He's determined to silence his critics and regain the respect of Mireille, who is taking her first successful steps in the film industry.

'Is that when you decide to go up a weight class?'

'Yes, I go up to bantamweight and challenge the Panamanian reigning world champion, Al Brown, or Panama, as he's known.'

Panama – a magnificent dandy who loves champagne, flashy cars and pretty girls, and is said to change outfits five times a day. Like Victor, he has known poverty and retained the soul of a child. The fight descends into parody. Al Brown is far too strong. It's a walk in the park for the Panamanian, but for Victor, it's a humiliation. It's also the beginning of the agonies of his love life.

'With Mireille, I became too jealous and possessive. I didn't realize that this attitude was taking me further and further away from the woman I love. It's all my fault.'

'You can't say that.'

Alfred notices a tear running down Young's hollow cheek as he gently lowers his head.

'I'm boring you with my stories.'

'Go on, Victor . . .'

'After that, it was the road to hell. I got bogged down in pathetic fights that were lost in advance.'

Victor tells him that this is when the film director Julien Duvivier chooses Mireille to appear with Jean Gabin in *Pépé le Moko*. Then it's *Gueule d'amour* (Lady Killer) and *Naples au baiser de feu* (The Kiss of Fire) with Tino Rossi, a huge star.

'As soon as I saw them together at rehearsals, I knew they were having an affair.'

'Did you have any evidence?'

'No, but when I insisted, Mireille confessed. Two days later she ditched me. It was a knock-out blow. I was a wreck.'

Without his friends – he says so himself – he might not still be alive. Friends who always thought that this woman had been toying with him, had never really loved him. The little Mozart of boxing had to sell his house; he lived in hotels, dragging his miserable self to the Coupole or the fashionable jazz clubs. In the Bœuf sur le Toit or the Tabou, he tries to forget Mireille by getting drunk on the sounds of Bill Coleman, Roy Eldridge, Frankie Newton and Duke Ellington. Jazz soaks up all his sadness.

As he listens to Younkie pouring out his sorrows, Alfred thinks of the words of a Cheikh Raymond song that he has never forgotten. *J'ai été ensorcelé par le tatouage de sa jambe entrevu sous l'anneau encerclant sa cheville. Comme l'amour succombe à un regard, comme l'infortune blesse par un dard, on m'a décoché une flèche fatale dont je ne peux pas guérir.* (I was enchanted by the tattoo on her leg, glimpsed below the bracelet encircling her ankle. As love succumbs to a look, as misfortune wounds with a dart, I was shot by a fatal arrow and I cannot recover from it.)

And then, rousing Alfred from his daydreams, Young recalls his staggering fight in Berlin on 10 November 1938.

'But what got into you that day?' Alfred cries passionately.

'Financially, I was in dire straits, you understand?'

For a small fee, for peanuts, Victor Young Perez accepts a gala match against the Austrian boxer Ernst Weiss. The Nazis want revenge for Max Schmeling's defeat at the hands of the black American boxer Joe Louis. Victor is unaware of everything that had happened during the night, but when he arrives at the train station he understands. All the streets are full of broken glass, looted shops, smashed doors, synagogues reduced to ashes. *Kristallnacht . . .*

Yet he goes to fight that very evening, under a barrage of spitting and insults. 'An end of the world atmosphere,' he tells Alfred. 'Frenzied SS men who'd come to witness the execution of a Jew. I throw all my strength into the fight, but an uppercut to the chin shatters me. I'm beaten on points. Leaving the ring is a nightmare, believe me.'

Eighteen months later, the whole of France is overrun. Like most of his friends, Victor is unsure about whether to return to Tunisia but, despite the occupation and the threats against the Jews, he wants to believe that his previous achievements offer him protection. He doesn't register, refuses to wear the yellow star, claims he's Spanish when suspicious eyes anatomize him from head to toe. He watches Marcel Cerdan's winning match against Gustave Humery, nicknamed the Killer. 'During that time,' he sighs, 'Mireille left Tino Rossi for a handsome German officer, Birl Desbok. When you look at the photos of them in the newspapers, they seem very much in love.'

Alfred knows only too well what comes next. It's the same story all over France. On 21 September 1943, three militiamen knock on Victor's door. Despite his explanations, he's carted off, interrogated and taken to the Drancy internment camp. As more and more people were rounded up, he had been on the point of organizing his escape from the area, along with several friends.

'We all had appointments with a doctor who had a reputation for bribing French and German officials, a certain Doctor Petiot . . .'[24]

At Drancy, Victor is immediately recognized by both the detainees and the guards. Everyone calls him 'champion'.

'I got that too,' Alfred says with a smile.

'To kill the boredom and anxiety, I gave some boxing demonstrations. Same as here. And then on 7 October, I was taken by coach to Bobigny station.'

Victor Young Perez looks up, his eyes still misty with tears.

'The end of the story is best forgotten.'

Paris, June 1940

After spending several months at the military training school in Joinville, in a unit for top-level sportsmen, Alfred is conscripted into the French Air Force. Like all his comrades, he's ready to do his duty. He's sent to Sétif, in Algeria, to serve in the Aïn Arnat battalion, leaving Paule behind in Paris for a time. However, his status as a swimmer means he is not sent to the front. After he's demobilized, he returns to the capital, to the relief of all his family in Constantine.

But not for long. The worst happens without warning. Blitzkrieg, German tanks crossing the frontlines at full speed, heading for Paris and destroying everything in their path. And then the devastating news that Alfred's little brother, Roger, has been killed in action. Just like that, in a second, one of thousands of other anonymous victims of a wave of machine gun fire. *Roger wouldn't have known anything about it . . .*

After the loss of his mother, who died so young, Alfred

feels as if a part of him has been blown away. When he looks at Roger in the photo of the three of them in uniform, the boys of the family, posing proudly and grinning, he feels as if he's looking at his twin. His double. Alfred thinks again of the prayer his father so often recited: *May God console us and the other mourners of Zion and Jerusalem*. He repeats it over and over, without really quite believing it.

Above the Arc de Triomphe, in a suddenly deserted city, the Nazi flag flutters in the wind. Barely four years ago, all the nations paraded before Hitler in a packed stadium in Berlin. And now they're on their knees. Like everyone in France, Alfred heard the quavering voice of Marshal Pétain on the radio, telling them to give way and obey the Germans. 'For your own good,' Pétain said. Maybe, who knows, it could even be a new beginning. The beginning of the nightmare, for sure: Alfred knows that for the Jews, obeying the Nazis means agreeing to disappear. To be obliterated.

At the Racing Club swimming pool, the atmosphere is awful. Despite his setbacks, Carton seems to be in a dreamlike mood, acting as if he had won the match. Alfred is aware of the directors having secret meetings behind his back. There are whisperings, mutterings, sly comments that make him feel uneasy.

'Things are going to get difficult for you, Alfred,' says Georges, his coach, confidingly. 'The Jews are in their sights, you'll have to play it safe.'

At home, Paule also urges him to be careful: 'Don't talk about the situation, don't clown around, swim more and more, better and better, that's your best protection.'

But in several newspapers, the threats are more and more unambiguous, the tone is direct, the words are spoken out loud. *Au pilori*, a journal that describes itself as a 'weekly fighting against the Judeo-masonic conspiracy', is among the most virulent. In the anteroom of his office on the Quais d'Aubervilliers, where they sometimes play tarot in the evenings, Émile, who no longer conceals his anxiety, hands Alfred an article. 'Can we reasonably allow a Jew to represent France in international competitions?' Alfred reads. Stunned, he drops the paper.

'They won't succeed, the swine,' says Émile.

'Yes, they will, my friend, the wheels have been set in motion.'

On 7 October 1940, Alfred's fears are confirmed: the Crémieux Decree, the law granting French citizenship to the Algerian Jews, is abolished. With a single stroke of a pen, he's nothing, neither French nor Algerian. Jewish, unwelcome everywhere. The final blow comes when he receives an official letter from the Ministry of Education. In words that cut like the blade of a guillotine, the government informs him that after the adoption of the Law on the Status of Jews, he no longer has the right to pursue his profession of sports teacher – the only thing that matters to him, the job that is even more precious than all his trophies put together. *I don't know anything better . . .*

The next day, it's Paule's turn to receive this insulting letter. That evening, curled up together on the blue sofa that faces the large windows of their living room, lost in the noisy bustle of the boulevard, there is nothing left to say to one another. Just a few tears that slip down their cheeks.

In their letters, Alfred's parents fear for him. For Paule and for themselves too, for their cousins, for their friends scattered around Algeria. David, Alfred's father, is afraid of being laid off. Rose says she's fearful from morning to night. There too, insults are increasing in the streets and the markets. They come from the Arabs who have long been up in arms against the Jews, but also, in a new twist, from openly antisemitic French people. Even children are pointing at them.

January 1941

'You really must leave this time, Alfred. Paris is too dangerous,' sighs Georges Hermant, meticulously arranging his copies of the *Miroir des Sports* on his bookshelves.

'But where should I go?'

Hermant smiles, relights his cigarette and takes him by the shoulder.

'To Toulouse, my boy, to our friends at the Dauphins swimming club. They're the best, after us. I've told Alban Minville, the coach, and he'd be delighted to welcome you there.'

Leave Paris. So it's that bad. As Alfred leaves Hermant's office, he's filled with anxiety. Why is it so urgent? What does Georges know that he daren't tell him? He learns the truth two days later from Georges's assistant, the charming, irreplaceable Mademoiselle Mercier.

'I haven't said anything to you, Alfred, but Jacques Cartonnet is an editor at an antisemitic journal. He has easy access everywhere, in particular to the Commissariat General for Jewish Affairs. He's spying on you, making note of your actions and movements, gathering information on your relationships and what you're reading. Monsieur Hermant is right, it's much too dangerous.'

Nothing this woman with the pretty white chignon whispers to him comes as a surprise. It confirms all his suspicions. For several weeks, the antisemites have been using sport as proof for the theory of the inequality of the races. As 'clumsy oafs or ungainly weaklings', according to sports journalist Jean Dauven, Jews are judged to be ill-suited to playing sports: 'Too weak physically and morally spineless. Natural enemies of physical effort and totally devoid of courage, which is not a virtue of their race.' Moreover, Dauven notes, 'There are no Jews, or almost none, among the great champions.' Or almost none . . . The achievements of Nakache and Victor Perez contradict this.[25] Yes, it's time to leave. Try to build a life somewhere safe from the Gestapo. Join a new team of swimmers. Get to know this city they say is gentle and warm. 'Down there, they call it *la ville rose*, the pink city,' Mademoiselle Mercier tells him. You'll be all right there with Paule. Take care or yourself, my boy.' *La ville rose* . . . Alfred tries to convince himself that a name like that must be a good omen.

★ ★ ★

Émile accompanied them onto the station platform. He came to pick them up at the Boulevard de Sébastopol early in the morning in his smart Citroën Traction Avant, with his little round glasses planted firmly on his nose. Émile puts on his usual cheerful manner, but Alfred, being well acquainted with him, knows that deep down his heart is bleeding. *He too is trying to hide his pain.* The pain of two friends parting. Paule and Alfred leave with almost nothing. They've entrusted Émile with their nice Simca 5. Officially, Artem is going to Toulouse to take a swimming course. In the car, they remain silent, aware of the roadblocks, of people looking at them. Émile tries to find the best route, but is held up by roadworks.

'We'll get there, don't worry.'

They almost don't. They reach the station just fifteen minutes before the train is due to depart. Émile and Alfred carry the two big suitcases. No time for effusive farewells, it's devilishly cold. *When will we see each other again, Émile?*

Toulouse – The Dolphins

In the magnificent pools of the TOEC Toulouse, on the Ile du Grand-Ramier in the heart of the city – two indoor pools for the winter and one outdoor pool 150 metres in length, the biggest in Europe – things move fast. The members of the Dauphins swimming club live up to their name: these 'dolphins' swim like fish and are crazy about training. Alfred remembers Fabien, the soldier at the Sidi M'Cid pool in Constantine who had swept away his fears. He had told Alfred about this club that had trained him and that he'd loved so much. Here, the pool is always swirling, with the energetic strokes of the swimmers creating a light, regular swell that makes it feel like you're swimming in the sea. What Alfred finds most striking is the strong friendship that seems to bind all the athletes together. They encourage one another in the water, give each other advice, meet up on one or two evenings a week at Bibent, the posh brasserie on the Place du Capitole. A group of buddies, welded together by the team spirit that Minville calls for in his gravelly voice with unshakeable faith. Minville, the supreme butterfly specialist, the man who came up with a whole new approach to the stroke. What a contrast with the Racing Club in Paris and its atmosphere poisoned by rivalry and contempt under the guise of the warlike nature of competition. On the first day there, Alfred feels good – very good, even.

'You're a fighter, Alfred. Your strength is in your muscles, but especially in your head.' Minville doesn't attempt to correct Alfred's style – which is what most sports journalists are obsessed with, overflowing with lyricism when it comes to describing the bodily movements of athletes – but instead tries to rebalance his body, or even to twist it, in order to produce the maximum speed. *He sees me as a sprinter.* He has devised a training programme for Alfred based on 100-metre sessions, including 25 metres underwater, 25 metres butterfly, 25 metres classic breaststroke, 25 metres butterfly, and then 25 metres while holding his breath.

After the lengths in the pool, Minville subjects him to a good two hours of strength training. It's anything but a punishment – Alfred doesn't know which he prefers, the swimming or the pommel horse. He also adores the rings, his arms stretched to loosen the joints. These sessions of gentle torture take place under the benevolent protection of the Jany family, who look after everything here: maintaining the water quality, cleaning the changing rooms and the gymnasium, taking care of the park and its century-old trees. The Janys live in a little house by the entrance to the sports centre, on the Ile du Ramier. Their son Alex is entering his first competitions. At the age of sixteen, he already radiates wonderful confidence. *That boy will certainly go far.* Katie, Alex's mother, takes great care of Paule. She gives her tours around the city, advises her on the best shops, shows her where to walk along the Garonne river. She also treats Alfred with motherly affection – the mother he lost, the kind and gentle words that make life sweet.

The Janys draw their attention to a gymnasium called the Académie, whose director is preparing to step down. It's on the Rue Philippe-Féral, right in the centre of the city. For Paule and Alfred, who are both qualified teachers of sport and physical education, it's a godsend – a way of earning their keep and for Alfred, a way of ensuring that he's always in top form. Minville and the directors of the swimming club support Alfred's application. The place is magnificent: a former workshop set over three floors, with brick walls and a steel frame, nice high ceilings and large windows overlooking the Grand-rue Nazareth. There isn't a lot of equipment, but there's enough. Watched by Paule and the Janys, Alfred shinnies up the knotted climbing rope in just four moves and touches the ceiling. All that remains is for him to stick out his tongue at his friends like a clown.

In the spring of 1941, they are really happy – a nice flat,

the gym that is always busy and which provides Alfred with an opportunity to regularly mix with members of the Jewish community in Toulouse. And especially Paule, who comes home one evening, throws herself into his arms, touches her little rounded tummy and without taking her eyes off him says: 'You're going to be a dad, Alfred. The baby's due at the beginning of September.'

There they are, focused on each other, embracing as they did on the first day. The world is theirs. They're intoxicated by this future that some people, believing they hear German boots approaching, would reduce to an enchanted interlude. First thing the next day Alfred sends his parents a telegram: 'A little Nakache should be appearing soon. A little champion, still in its bubble of water, who sends you lots of kisses. From your loving Alfred.'

He also phones Émile to tell him the good news. It does him good to hear his friend's high-pitched voice and rapid-fire delivery. Émile is happy for them: 'How lucky you are to be living in the sunshine of Toulouse! Paris is just a shadow of its former self. The curfew, the German patrols and all the things you know about, Alfred.'

He doesn't say any more, as he's anxious not to spoil Alfred's happiness. Alfred knows that without naming them, Émile is talking about the ever more numerous anti-Jewish measures resulting from the collaboration, and that he is urging him to be cautious.

'Don't worry, Émile, I have good people around me here and I'm protected by our minister, Jean Borotra.'

'That's good, Alfred, keep being successful in the pools, I want titles.' Émile laughs his childlike laugh before hanging up.

It's true, after all, that with Jean Borotra – formerly one of the 'Four Musketeers' of the French national tennis team, the 'Bounding Basque', the respected general commissioner for education and sport – Alfred isn't risking much. *Swim, Alfred, swim and don't brood too much.* In May, a phone call from the commissioner's office confirms that Émile was right: Borotra suggests that Alfred should join the French squad that is going to North Africa for a prestige tour by the flag-bearers of French sport. He feels as if he's been given a ticket to his lost paradise. While travelling through Algeria, he'll see all his family. The only downside is that Paule won't be able to accompany him because she's pregnant. Katie Jany reassures him: she'll be with her and, if she wants to, Paule could even move into their little house at the edge of the sports centre park.

Auschwitz – In the name of the brother

Once again, Gérard from Marseille has permission to go to the Auschwitz III infirmary. He has insisted on getting treatment for a bad wound on his hand. However, his sole aim is to spend some time with Nakache. Gérard is still on his feet. He's not taking a big risk by undergoing the regular selection process carried out in the treatment rooms. The method is always the same: lean forward with your legs apart, while the Nazi doctor measures the size of your buttocks. If they're too thin, it's the gas chamber. How many detainees who go in thinking they're going to be given some medicine or a compress have signed their own death warrants? He had been given permission to go to the infirmary by his block-leader, an extremely sadistic Flemish ex-convict, who chose him – he has never understood why – to be his cleaner and serve up the evening ration to the detainees. As part of his job doing the leader's washing-up, he's allowed to eat any leftovers.

Like the others, Gérard has been mouldering in the same pyjamas ever since he arrived at Monowitz and is constantly struggling against the lice. However, he takes particular care to wash himself with snow every day. Thanks to this discipline and the extra food, he keeps up the best appearance possible. On this day, however, he doesn't want to talk to Alfred about himself or Marseille, but about his big brother, Pierre, who continues to decline.

'I don't know what to do any more, he's lost interest in everything, has no energy.'

'Are you able to talk to him about it?'

'Less and less. I think he wants to end it all.'

Alfred recognizes this state of depression in detainees who, for some strange reason, are known in the camp as *Muslims*. He knows that no one and nothing will succeed in giving these people back an ounce of vitality, still less any hope.

'Keep talking to him about your childhood, your roller-skating races in Marseille, the girls you used to ogle on the beach. Talk to him, even if it's no use any more.'

No use, indeed. A few days later, Gérard sees Pierre return to the infirmary in pain. He says his foot was crushed by a tipper truck. He goes straight to selection. In a toneless voice, Gérard tells Alfred, who hadn't been there: 'I saw Pierre leave from the wrong side of the infirmary. He was stark naked, thrown into a lorry like a sack. He gave me a little wave, as if he wanted to make me understand that this was a deliverance. And that one of us needed to stay alive to one day report what goes on here.'

June 1941 – Back to the roots

In the twin-engine jet transporting them above the clouds, Alfred is seated next to two athletes whose achievements he was familiar with but whom he had never met before: Jean Lalanne, the star long-distance runner and French 10,000 metre champion, a true son of the Pyrenees who grew up near Toulouse, in Bagnères-de-Bigorre, and Marcel Hansenne, originally from Roubaix in the north, the French outdoor champion at 800 metres.

Like Alfred, Marcel will be visiting Casablanca, one of the biggest cities in Morocco, on the Atlantic coast, for the first time. Alfred tells him about Algeria, about the charm of the casbahs, the unreal beauty of the Rhumel Gorges and the thermal pool where he learned to swim and overcome his fear of the water. He also talks about the spring festival where Jews and Arabs distil orange-flower water and rosewater – his favourite childhood festival and the most cheerful of them all. Everyone there called it *la journée rose*, or rose day.

'After buying bags of white flowers and rose petals in the market, we bring the copper still up from the cellar and we collect the extracts in houses flooded with scents.'

'And what do you do with them?'

'The rosewater is used for washing and dressing. The orange-flower water is for sweetening coffee and flavouring pastries. But it's also part of our religious festivals. It's what we call "the water of good fortune". You should have seen my grandmother sprinkling it over the faithful as they left the synagogue . . .'

Marcel is eager to experience this oriental atmosphere, so different from what he has known up till then. Alfred's Jewishness doesn't seem to bother him, quite the opposite. To be honest, he hasn't even thought about it. In turn, he is keen to talk about his home region – less sophisticated, maybe, certainly less sunny, but still so warm, he says. 'The sun we don't have above our heads,' he says with a smile, 'is in our hearts.' As they fly over the Mediterranean, he tells him about old Roubaix, with its *courées* – the narrow alleys of red brick workers' houses – and its amazing swimming pool, built about ten years ago.

'Do you know this pool, Alfred?'

'I've heard about it, like everyone, but I've never swum there.'

'It was based on the design of an abbey, goodness knows why. The big pool is like a nave with stained glass windows on either side, representing the rising and setting sun. It's magnificent. And most importantly, it's the only place where middle-class children and kids from the streets can meet.'

Marcel is as chatty as he is fond of his part of the world. After the pool, its stained glass and its 'swimmers' refectory', he describes the welcoming taverns where the miners drink themselves silly, singing songs in Ch'ti, the Picard language of north-eastern France, at the tops of their voices. And this Northerner turned Parisian starts singing: *Dors, min p'tit quinquin, min p'tit pouchin, min gros rojin* . . . ('Sleep, my little child, my little chick, my plump grape'). Alfred has heard this song before, but didn't know that it was the rallying cry for all the Ch'tis in France. Seated in front of them, Borotra, seeing his athlete transforming into a music-hall star, turns around with a big smile: 'Well, I see these two are going to get on like a house on fire . . .'

On the other side of the aisle, Marcel Cerdan, a promising young boxer, applauds. It's quite the start for a trip that makes them forget the pressure of competition and, even more, the wounded country of France, one half under the Nazi yoke and the remainder run by a quavering old marshal.

The ululations of Casablanca are succeeded by those of Algiers, long awaited, where the entire Nakache clan has assembled to celebrate the return of the hero. *The infinite happiness of reunions* . . . In the stands of the pool of la

Sablette, in the heart of the Bay of Algiers, a huge crowd has arrived to watch the local boy swim.

Men, women and children, they all arrived very early on a beautifully sunny day. Alfred can hear them from the changing rooms, whistling impatiently and chanting his name. A group of women point out the organizer of the event, waving a placard saying: 'Alfred, we love you!' Alfred savours this moment that precedes their entering the arena, while also regretting that Paule and his unborn child cannot be there. How he would have loved his son or daughter to be present at the return of the child prodigy amid this outpouring of love. The loudspeakers brutally interrupt his reveries.

'Mesdames, messieurs, please give a triumphal welcome to our great champion, Alfred Nakache, one of the best swimmers in the world!'

When he enters the arena, the crowd rise to their feet as one. His parents and brothers lead the cheering, as do his teammates, magnificent in their white uniforms with the French flag emblem sewn on the chest. He mounts the starting block, sticks out his tongue, then, without even focusing first, dives straight into the cool water. He hadn't planned on breaking any records at this gala demonstration, but his taste for speed takes over: he gives it his all, arms, chest and legs in overdrive, justifying his reputation as the fighter of the pools. On leaving the water, he does a front flip on the wet ground as they cheer. Rose, who is like a mother to him, throws herself into his arms, to the popping of flashbulbs. Alfred feels as if he has just scored a lucky goal in the last minute of a Red Star match. The goal of liberation and victory.

That evening, the family has organized a dinner with a few friends under the arcades of the Bay of Algiers. There's a lot of joking and laughter. Maybe too much, as if they were exorcizing a feeling of uncertainty, of fragility. Little by little, Alfred withdraws from the conversation. His grandmother Sarah, seated on his left and wearing her pretty traditional Judeo-Arab dress, senses it. She takes his hand. She's no longer very strong and her eyesight is gradually failing. She whispers in his ear: 'Alfred, keep the feast-days deep in your heart for the testing times.' *What are you talking about, Granny?*

Auschwitz – Swim faster than death

Willy Holt, like all the detainees in Auschwitz whose talents interest the Nazis, benefits from favourable treatment. The young painter had the great idea of producing erotic sketches. In light of the success of his work, and by popular demand, he moves shamelessly into pornography. As a result, he gets to sleep in the infirmary and has access to better food. His imagination knows no bounds when it comes to making the staff fantasize. For Officer Strauss, who had suggested the idea, he came up with a special comic strip, in which a soldier, on all fours and with his trousers pulled down around his knees, is whipped by a dominatrix.

The Boche is evidently delighted with his reading matter, but he could just as easily have been annoyed, got into a rage and sent Willy back to the hell of the barracks. Or killed him with a shot in the head, while laughing loudly. That was the fate met by Axel, a homosexual contortionist, who was guilty of getting just a bit too close to the camp commandant during a demonstration of his skills. After the show, with their lit cigars still in their mouths, they threw him outside and killed him with several volleys of machine gun fire.

Like Willy, Alfred feels like he's walking a tightrope. The slightest thing can cause you to lose your balance. But he doesn't resign himself to the situation. The anger boiling within him is too strong to give up. There are some humiliations he just has to accept, because even with his champion's aura, to do otherwise would mean risking death. The dagger test, when that officer made him dive for a knife in the murky pool, remains in him like a blade that pierces his heart. But inwardly the memory strengthens him, makes him want to live and fight.

This is how it comes to pass that, one Sunday in July, Alfred suggests a crazy idea to a young detainee, sixteen-year-old Noah Klieger: to go and dive into the water tank used for putting out fires. *And swim, swim, and keep swimming.* At the risk of being shot in the water without warning, just to swim without acting like circus animals for SS men wanting a show. *Just cut through the water. Feel free.*

Noah loves the idea of defying their guards. He's a very good swimmer. Artem is particularly impressed by his nerve. The previous evening, behind a lorry outside the infirmary, this lad with the broad forehead and bright eyes had told him about his dare-devil childhood. He grew up in Strasbourg,

Luxembourg and Antwerp, in Belgium, under the harsh authority of his father, Abraham, a journalist and writer descended from a family of Polish Jews. At school, Noah was aggressive and undisciplined, but also very bright. He was moved up a class several times, and at the age of eleven he devoured Dostoyevsky, Tolstoy and Victor Hugo, read poems by Schiller, Goethe and Byron, which he didn't quite understand, but that didn't matter. At secondary school, he became a member of the Renards, a young Zionist group that excelled at sport – football, swimming and dodgeball – and folk dance – hora and cherkessia.

In May 1940, forced to flee from the advancing Germans, he walked for ten days with his family all the way to Dunkirk, under fire from the *Stukas*, the awful dive bombers that swoop down vertically, sowing death as they pass with sirens howling like hyenas. 'After that, when you get through it,' he confides to Alfred, 'you feel you're invincible.' Standing on the beach, Noah watched the evacuation of the British troops under a hail of German bombs. Then he and his parents were taken back to Antwerp by the Wehrmacht and, a few months later, like hundreds of foreign Jews, they were transferred to the small Belgian city of Genk. There, his father Abraham was arrested by the Gestapo and sent to the Breendonk concentration camp.

'I tried everything I could think of,' says Noah with a smile. 'I wrote a long letter to General von Falkenhausen, the military governor of Belgium and Northern France, telling him that my father was not a criminal and that my mother was very ill.'

'You must be crazy!' exclaims Alfred.

'Weeks later I was summoned to the headquarters of the Gestapo. I was taken to the office of a superior officer who said: "Who do you think you are? How dare you write to the Military Governor." I explained my situation and he replied in an incomprehensible language. Then he said: "What? Don't you even understand the language of your people? You don't understand Hebrew? Doesn't it seem strange to you that you, a Jew, don't know your language, whereas I, a German officer, can speak it?" I stammered that yes, it was a bit odd, even though I could make out a few words of Hebrew I'd heard in prayers. Then he said: "I learned Hebrew in Palestine, where I grew up. Now, get out, I've wasted enough time on you." I'd just spotted his name and rank on his office door: *Sturmbannführer* Joachim Erdmann.'

'What happened next?'

'You won't believe it: a fortnight later, my father came home, bald and thinner. General von Falkenhausen had acceded to my request. A miracle.'

The sound of boots a few metres away makes then jump. A group of soldiers has stopped for a smoke a bit further along the wall. Alfred and Noah fall silent, holding their breath in air polluted by the smell of cigarettes. The soldiers talk loudly, burst out laughing and then leave. Noah immediately resumes his story.

After rescuing his father, he joined an underground network, known as Le Pionnier, that smuggled people to Switzerland and helped to exfiltrate dozens of young Jews. On 15 October 1942, in the face of increasing danger, he decided it was his turn to escape from Belgium. However, three men in black leather coats burst into the little bistro in Mouscron where he was sipping a beer while he waited for the smuggler. They checked people's ID, left, then came back into the little restaurant.

'One of them,' says Noah, 'came over to me and said: "Come to the toilets with me." I asked him why. "I want to check if you're Jewish." I knew the end had come.'

'What did you do?'

'I replied in German: "No need to check. I am indeed a Jew, just as you're a damned German. And you won't win the war anyway and Nazi Germany will be destroyed." The Gestapo men showed me what they thought of my predictions with punches and kicks.'[26]

When he arrived at Auschwitz, Noah lost none of this spontaneous fighting spirit. He raised his hand when they asked the detainees if any of them were good boxers, even though he'd never worn a pair of gloves before. How could he prove it? 'In a corner of the room set aside for training,' he tells Alfred, 'I saw Victor Young Perez shadowboxing, throwing jabs and hooks. I copied him as best I could, afraid that I looked like a dancer in a nightclub. But they believed me – another minor miracle.' *This lad*, thinks Alfred, *is definitely not like all the rest.*

* * *

With that kind of incredible audacity, it's no wonder that Noah is delighted by Alfred's suggestion on this Sunday. Together they set up a warning system: accomplices placed at strategic points around the tank alert them of the arrival of any patrols. They are Léon, Gérard, Victor Perez, and also Charles, a young architecture student who dreams of winning the Prix de Rome. Alfred calls these lookouts his 'dolphins', or sometimes 'the Francophones', because they all speak French. Without a moment's hesitation, Alfred and Noah take off their pyjamas and jump straight into the water. *God, that's good . . .* Alfred starts swimming the crawl slowly. *Wouldn't want to humiliate Noah . . .* Under the eye of their protectors, they cover about ten lengths there and back before stopping for a few minutes at the edge of the tank.

Noah and Alfred make this illusion of happiness last as long as possible. They want to prove to themselves that they're still men. 'By doing this, Noah, we're showing that we still have human feelings. We're not just numbers. It's encouraging for the others. So, if you like, we'll do it again.'

In the water, Noah sticks up his thumb as a sign of approval. In the evening, some of the detainees ask them to tell them all about these crazy excursions, as if they were talking about an escape.

Or a journey to the end of the world.

World record

Back in Toulouse, reinvigorated by his trip south, Alfred starts training again with all the energy of an adolescent. He has become a true member of the Dolphins, the leader of a wonderfully close-knit team. They all have their sights set on the international meeting in Marseille on 6 July 1941, where the world's best in each discipline are expected. The home of the local élite swimming club, the Cercle des nageurs de Marseille, with its pool hollowed out of a rocky outcrop plunging into the sea, is a splendid venue. Alban Minville has put Nakache down for the 200 metres butterfly. His rival is the previously unbeaten American Jack Kasley. But Alban wants to believe. Puffing on his umpteenth cigarette, he assures Alfred in his stentorian voice: 'Marseille is like home for you. With the crowd urging you on, it'll be like swimming with flippers.'

'If you say so.'

He was right, that day is ten times as exciting as Algiers

was. A manic atmosphere. In the clear water of the pool, galvanized by the waves of encouragement, Artem is not just one of the dolphins but a shark cutting through the foam. He ignores Kasley and his incredible record of achievements. His only enemy is himself: Artem overcoming Alfred. *The fighter pitted against the wimp.* He had never had the feeling of swimming this fast before. Raising his head from the foaming water in a daze, he stares at the men with the stopwatches. The judges consult each other, looking flabbergasted, and suddenly the announcer yells through the megaphone: 'Record beaten! Record beaten! World record smashed in 2 minutes 37 seconds!' Alfred needs time, quite some time, to recover his wits and realize that this isn't a joke. Fair play, Jack Kasley gives him a friendly wave. Alfred is now one of the fastest breaststroke swimmers in the world.

Carton is sulking. Carton, whose French hundred-metre butterfly record Alfred had taken from him the previous weekend, with a time of 1 minute 9.3 seconds. Jean Borotra sends Alfred a congratulatory message the same evening, and so does André Haon, the mayor of Toulouse, a true sports lover, a former rugby player and the president of the Toulouse stadium. In addition, there are messages from Hermant, his coach at the Racing Club in Paris, and from the charming Mademoiselle Mercier. The great majority of the press applaud him. A journalist at *L'Auto* writes words he finds touching: 'This record is the symbol of a life in which anything can be achieved through courage.' At the hotel Les Bords de Mer, where the swimmers are staying, Alfred spends long minutes on the phone with Paule. She has followed the competition in the French news together with the Janys. He asks her for news of the baby she's expecting. 'Your future offspring is fine, Alfred. You may not want to believe it, but during the race I felt as if he was kicking along with you.' *Paule is like that, she gives life to life.* Two months later, on 12 August, little Annie beams at them with the most beautiful smile.

★ ★ ★

For Jean Borotra, the North-African tour was one tour too many. Émile had warned Alfred in his letters: all of Paris is buzzing with the news of the impending dismissal of the Bounding Basque. What Émile doesn't tell Alfred is that it's entirely, or almost entirely, because of him. Now, at the beginning of 1942, Borotra is being openly reprimanded for having taken Nakache with him. A Jew on an official tour, whatever next? Alfred shouldn't have relied on his achievements and his reputation as a great champion, remembering that he's now a pariah. In the columns of *Au Pilori*, the attacks grow ever stronger: 'As for this fantastic, marvellous, extraordinary swimmer, this supernatural man, this demi-god with the curly hair and the flared nostrils, as they like to depict him in a big Parisian daily? He's the Jew Artem Nakache, a member of the Zionist Maccabi movement.'

In April, Borotra is unceremoniously sacked by the Vichy government. He has fled and the Gestapo are hot on his heels. Nakache has lost his protector and in Toulouse, once-friendly faces are changing. Will his friends at the Dauphins club turn their backs on him too? Abandon him? Denounce him? *Suppose there were to be another Cartonnet hiding in this lovely group of friends?* The idea terrifies him. At training, Alfred sounds out his mates, tries to detect the slightest whisper on their lips, a hint of irony. But there's nothing, just beaming smiles and open, friendly embraces. It's as if they were creating a bubble around him, aware of the dangers that threaten him.

He also feels safe in the gym. Some people pump iron or swing around the pommel-horses, while others climb the ropes or pull themselves up on the rings, in a skilfully anarchic ballet. The room smells of sweat and leather, of the energy and passion of living. Among the regulars is Aaron Stein, a recently dismissed maths teacher. Behind one of the big steel columns that support the structure, he tells Alfred about the underground war he is waging with several friends from the département of Lot-et-Garonne. The group they've formed is called the Jewish Army. A network for resistance, sabotage and counter-attack.

'Help us, Alfred, to make ourselves into real fighters,' Aaron whispers in his ear. 'You're the only one who can prepare us for the confrontation.'

'I don't know anything about combat sports, but I can install a ring and start a boxing section.'

'Do you have anyone in mind to run it?'

'Yes, I have an idea.'

Félix Lebel is a former boxer from a boxing club in the region, the Amicale pugilistique de la Garonne. Now retired from the ring, he's a decorator by day and a poker-player by night, in the back room of his shop. Félix often comes along at the weekend to watch Alfred swim, and Alfred sometimes joins him for a game of cards. He'll put the gloves on again for Alfred.

Auschwitz – Sharing

In the camp where people are dying of starvation and even more of despair, Alfred feels almost ashamed when he receives a parcel one day in the presence of Robert Waitz and Willy Holt.

'It's from the Red Cross,' says Robert. 'They've made enquiries and they know you're here among us.'

'But what about the Germans?'

'Don't forget, Alfred, that you're a swimming champion. They'll never consider you the same as the others. Even my medical qualifications, my haematology publications, my diplomas are worth nothing compared with your trophies. They've given their consent for you to receive this parcel.'

'I can't.'

'Open it, Alfred, or I'll do it for you.'

Alfred hesitates for a moment. He feels like the spoiled child of the *Krankenbau* – the infirmary. He hates this feeling. Even as a child, he couldn't bear the slightest injustice within the family, still less the teachers' pets who showed off in class. He thought they were contemptible. He also remembers Purim, the religious festival that was so important in Constantine. A joyful celebration demanding generosity towards others – sending food parcels and gifts to the poor.

Robert pulls the parcel towards him and authoritatively unties the string around it, revealing a small treasure trove: jam, biscuits, bars of chocolate, a huge ham and also ten cakes of soap – the supreme luxury.

'We'll divide it in four: one part for you, one for Noah, one for Willy,[27] and the last one for me.'

'Forget my share,' says Robert with a smile. 'Let me have a bar of soap and taste a bit of chocolate. Others are in urgent need.'

'I'm with you, Professor.'

Noah and Willy follow suit. So over the next few days, they divide up the Red Cross parcel into a multitude of little packages wrapped in paper. In order to bring these fleeting but precious crumbs of comfort to the most destitute inmates of the death camp, they'll have to avoid arousing the attention of the SS and the kapos, the prisoners assigned to supervise them. Nakache takes a parcel to block 35, where he is overcome with emotion when a man lying on a straw mattress caresses his hand. He is maybe forty or fifty years old, but his extreme thinness makes it impossible to tell his age. '*Yevarechecha HaShem*,' whispers the man. May the Lord bless you.

A few weeks later, Alfred receives a note from Willy, written on a scrap of paper rolled up in a cigarette. The writing is cramped, almost illegible. Alfred goes over to the triangle of light penetrating the room. He reads: 'The lesson in solidarity you taught me, my friend, will now be a rule of conduct for me. A crust of bread, simple potato peelings or a cigarette do little good physically, but the eyes of the recipient can light up with such a smile, such a glow of consolation, that one mustn't be held back by how commonplace the act may seem.'

In response, Alfred's face lights up with a bright smile.

Summer 1942

The atmosphere is heavy. It's not just the stifling heat beating down on the country. It's heavy with a dull anxiety. With its discriminatory measures against the Jews, the Vichy government is getting ahead of the demands of the Nazis. They're saying everywhere that foreign Jews are under threat – Jews from Germany and Eastern Europe who fled the pogroms and arrests and, after crossing Belgium, have come to seek refuge in the peaceful villages south of the Loire.

Maurice Hirsch, a member of the gym in Toulouse, is one of them. He has told Alfred his whole story. He left Leipzig with his family after *Kristallnacht* in autumn 1938. During that night of horror throughout the Reich, the SS set fire to synagogues, destroyed shops run by Jews and killed men, women and children. Nothing remained of the Hirsch family's shoe repair business but a pile of burnt wood. Now Maurice is sure that huge raids are being planned all over the

South of France. Thousands of foreign Jews will be deported to Germany and Poland. He's heard it from a friend, an agent of the Vichy Social Service.

Is he giving in to panic? Nakache isn't sufficiently well informed; he's too busy with his training and with running the gym to know. And then, to be honest, politics isn't his strong point. He's ashamed of the fact that many references in the discussions escape him. Towards the end of August, on Monday 23rd, Félix Lebel, Alfred's boxing assistant, comes into the gym. He looks preoccupied. He hands Alfred a letter from the Archbishop of Toulouse, Monsignor Saliège, which is due to be read in every parish. Félix is a practising Christian, and so is his wife Babeth. Every Sunday they attend the high mass at 11 o'clock in the cathedral of Saint-Pierre.

'Read that in peace tonight. It's brave, it's lovely, but it doesn't bode well.'

Alfred folds the sheet in four and stuffs it in the pocket of his tracksuit. Félix is like a brother to him. But the amateur boxer is already at the far end of the room, motivating his troops: 'Come on, boys, what are we waiting for? Hit the punching bags. Right, left, hook, and move your legs, for goodness sake!'

★ ★ ★

At home, Paule is the one who reads the archbishop's text. That day, Alfred doesn't touch the orange-flower pastries his wife has made but pours himself a large glass of Cahors wine, though he doesn't normally drink much. She sits down opposite him and starts reading aloud: 'My very dear brothers . . . that children, women, men, fathers and mothers are treated like cattle, members of the same family separated from one another and sent to an unknown destination, it has been reserved for our age to witness this sad spectacle . . .'

Paule pauses. In silence, she runs her eyes over the lines, then starts reading aloud again, making an effort to keep her voice clear.

'In our diocese, terrifying scenes have taken place in the Noé and Récébédou camps.[28] Jews are men and women. It is not permissible to do all these things against them, these men and women, these fathers and mothers. They are members of the human race. They are our brothers, like so many others. A Christian may not forget this . . . Shall I go on, Alfred?'

'Yes, finish it.'

'France, our beloved country, France who bears in the consciences of all your children the tradition of respect of the human being, I am sure you are not responsible for these horrors. Jules-Géraud Saliège, Archbishop of Toulouse.'

Alfred stands up as she folds up the piece of paper. She looks distant. He goes to stand behind her, plunges his hand into her beautiful dark hair and strokes the nape of her neck for a long time.

'Félix passed this on to me. I'm not sure that one man of the church alone can change things.'

'It's so humane, it will rouse people's conscience, at any rate.'

'I have my doubts, Paule.'

'Does it affect us?'

'Not directly. Not immediately. They're rounding up the foreign Jews. Only if they tell themselves that Algerian Jews are no longer French.'

'Is that the case?'

'On paper, yes, but I don't know what they're going to decide. Nobody knows.'

Can the outraged appeal of an archbishop be enough to restrain the zeal of the Vichy leaders? On 29 August, across the whole of southern France, the police wake up hundreds of families at dawn. They have five minutes, not one minute more, to fill a suitcase and get into a coach. Maurice Hirsch, his wife and his three children are arrested too. Where are they taken? Félix thinks he knows: to vast detention centres. Waiting for the train that will take them to Drancy, near Paris, and from there . . . This round-up is like a punch to the gut.

But at the gym, Aaron shows bullish determination: 'We'll fight, Alfred, like you do in the pool. Keep your distance from us, and above all, keep on swimming.'

Alfred likes Aaron's directness. There are several others like him who want to take up arms. They meet outside the city, in an isolated barn far from any houses, to put the finishing touches to their plans, practise shooting and write their leaflets. The Jewish Army. After the shameful arrests ordered by Marshall Pétain and his henchman Pierre Laval, the clandestine organization is living up to its name like never before.

Félix tells Alfred that in Lyon, the cardinal is also rebelling against this round-up. His name is Gerlier and he fights against the Prefect, Angeli, from morning to night. With the help of a priest, Father Glasberg, a Jew who converted to Catholicism, he is said to have succeeded in arranging the escape of a hundred or so children from an internment camp at Vénissieux, a suburb of Lyon, by making the parents sign acts of abandonment, relinquishing their legal rights as guardians, during the night. One of the girls is said to have had earrings in her pocket that her mother had left her. She'd promised never to lose them. At home, when Alfred tells Paule about this rescue operation, she is unable to hide her sadness.

'The kids have been sent to stay with families, Paule, they're in safety.'

'But the police must be looking everywhere for them?'

'Maybe, but they say that in Lyon there's incredible solidarity between believers and non-believers, Catholics, Jews, non-religious people, protestants. They form a kind of barricade. A cordon sanitaire. And on top of that, the resistance networks have been mobilized. They distribute leaflets in the city. Look, Félix gave me an example . . .'

In enormous capital letters, Paule reads the warning: 'You won't have the children.'[29]

* * *

For the inhabitants of Toulouse, November 1942 is a dark month. The Gestapo are in the streets of the city. It's the end of the *zone libre*, and the last illusions of the Nakaches have been shattered. According to the ninth decree of the 'occupation authorities', 'Jews are henceforth banned from all sporting events, whether as participants or spectators, as is access to the beaches and swimming pools.' The Nazis have set up their headquarters in the Hotel de l'Ours Blanc. Alfred has won five French championship titles[30] in recent months and the collaborationist press let fly at him, reproaching the directors of the French Swimming Federation for allowing him to take part in the competitions. One evening as Alfred is leaving the gym, a man with his hat pulled down over his eyes and his collar turned up approaches him. Alfred can't make out his face.

'What do you want with me?'

The man hands him a newspaper cutting.

'Here, read this and learn from it.'

By the time Alfred reaches a street light, the stranger has already disappeared into the dark, snow-covered streets of the neighbourhood. It's an article from the Pétainist newspaper *Pays libre* (Free Country), published under the byline 'P.L.' The man in black has underlined some passages in ballpoint pen.

SPORT IS A BEAUTIFUL THING

But the Jews must not have the honour of national competition.

IS NAKACHE A JEW?

If so, he must be excluded from competitions.

Last week we asked if Nakache is a Jew. And if he is, he should be excluded from sporting competitions. We have long campaigned against the Jews who have led our country to disaster, and that is why we insist again today and demand an inquiry into the world record holder and French champion: Nakache.

It would be a pity to see a Jew's name inscribed to represent France on the plaque of world records. So something must be done.

Is Nakache Jewish? We want answers. So explain yourself, Nakache!

But if you are Jewish, withdraw from French sport or you may well feel the consequences.

His heart misses a beat. For the first time, he feels an icy liquid run down his spine. Is that fear?

Toulouse, 1943

What is Jacques Cartonnet doing in Toulouse? The whole city is buzzing with the presence of the former champion from Paris. He can be seen everywhere with his Brylcreemed hair and long silhouette – at the city hall, at the prefecture and also at the *petit château*, the great bourgeois house in the Busca district which the Gestapo ended up preferring to the Hotel de l'Ours Blanc. It's because they needed more space for all their people. There are more and more of them, German officers but also zealous French civil servants, tracking down the supposed enemies of the Reich: members of the resistance, Jews, communists, homosexuals, artists, intellectuals – not forgetting the top-level sportsmen, worshipped by the public, who sometimes believe they can do anything. According to Félix, who is still well received by the local councillors, there's also a lot of partying going on at the little château.

'The top floor, you may not know, is something of

a brothel. A gathering of revellers who organize fine parties that go on all night long. It seems that Carton needs no introduction. He's right at home there. He's even one of the masters of ceremony.'

Alfred is, however, thunderstruck by what he learns: for several months, Carton has been running the youth and sports service of the Haute-Garonne militia. He has swapped his tweed jackets and flannel trousers for the fitted uniform of the henchmen of the Gestapo. The former dreamboat of the chic districts of Paris no longer shakes hands: he does the Nazi salute. And he attends propaganda parties where he proposes 'defining the role played by men's physical education and sport in the national revolution'. He is also now gunning for Alfred. Cartonnet, his former rival in the pool, wants Alfred's sporting death. *Maybe he even dreams of seeing me die* . . . As the French championships due to be held in Toulouse approach, the local papers, controlled by the Gestapo, unleash their fury. It's out of the question that an Algerian Jew should represent the city. The collaborationist organ *Je suis partout (I am everywhere)* drips with hatred and threats: 'Nakache is the least defensible of the Jews, the most specifically Yiddish Yid of all the Yids. A vile character who should at the very least be in a concentration camp . . .'

Early July 1943. In the middle of a training session, Alban Minville makes Alfred get out of the water. 'Get dressed and meet me in my office.'

Why the sinister look? Alfred has a bad feeling about this. For several weeks, the pressure has been too great. Cartonnet's men, swathed in their long raincoats, are keeping watch around the gym. They spy on the entrances and exits, make notes in their little notebooks, and drive off again at speed in their fancy saloons. Writing from Paris, Émile has confirmed that the repression of French Jews, no longer only of foreigners, is intensifying day by day, and tells Alfred that he should hide out in Spain. He and Paule have been thinking about it. One evening, they even joined a group that was preparing to cross the Pyrenees with a people smuggler. But Annie's crying would have risked scuppering everything. Above all, he has never imagined himself abandoning ship and leaving behind his team of Dolphins.

The other day, while he was having a coffee on the terrace of the brasserie Bibent, a man casually dropped a magazine onto his table on his way out. At first glance, it looked like a copy of *Match*, the popular magazine about the lives of the stars. But Alfred immediately realized that the magazine was a vile pastiche of the July 1938 issue of *Match*, which had featured a full-page picture of him on the back cover, smiling from ear to ear and with his tongue sticking out as usual.

Paule treasures that copy of *Match*, which celebrates Alfred's crop of titles: French championships and European records. The issue is dedicated to him. The authors of this piece of trash re-worked the original, distorted the photo of

Alfred, made his tongue more pointed, his eyes smaller and more sunken . . . and they changed the name of the magazine to *The Clowns of Sport, supplement to the magazine* Revivre, *the great illustrated magazine of race.*

Alfred leaned over to scan the article. The headline: *The idol of the Jewified swimming pools.* The text, written by Jean Dauven, was incredibly violent:

> We have to put an end to it. It is important to purge French sport of its Jews. Moreover, thanks to the general measures, this partial cleansing will be easier to achieve than one that would involve washing away the mercenary grime of French sport, through which the Jewish mindset, with all its cupidity and hypocrisy, still rules over our sport and keeps it in the mire.

Vehemently denouncing the lack of radical measures in the field of sport and the reprehensible complicity of the French Swimming Federation, Dauven continued: 'The Jews can still benefit from the same advantages and they don't miss any opportunity to make use of them. This is one of the rare occasions on which they can take off the clothes marked with the yellow star and be like everyone else.'

★ ★ ★

'Sit down, Alfred. What I have to say to you is not easy,' sighs Alban. 'The Germans are firmly opposed to your

participation in the French championships. Émile-Georges
Drigny[31] and the Federation have tried to protect you by
holding the event here in Toulouse, instead of in Paris, as
originally planned. There's nothing more they can do.'

'But . . .?'

'But your friends don't see it the same way. If you
don't have the right to compete, they will boycott the
competition.'

Alfred mumbles that he doesn't want them to miss what
they've been training for all year. Deep down, however, he
finds their decision heart-warming.

'They're going to decide individually, in all good
conscience. Despite the Gestapo's threats, those who join
the boycott won't be sanctioned by the club, I promise you
that, Alfred.'

Before returning to his flat, Alfred decides to drop into
the gym. He needs to clear his head, think of something else.
At the back of the room, he sees Aaron lifting weights. As he
catches sight of Alfred, he drops the bar with a thud.

'They've fired you, haven't they?'

'How did you guess, Aaron?'

'Our army has ears. That Cartonnet will have spared you
nothing. They're going to pursue you, Alfred. The situation
isn't just hot, it's burning.'

'I'm afraid I've already got my hands burned.'

The announcement that he has been excluded from the

championship has spread like wildfire throughout the city. At the brasserie Bibent, over a glass of white wine, Félix is confident: 'The people of Toulouse will show these bastards what they're made of. There will be loads of gaps in the stands. What are your Dolphins going to decide?'

'I won't ask anything of them, I don't want to put them in an awkward position.'

How long is it since Alfred laughed like a kid? And when was the last time he acted the clown, sticking out his tongue and rolling his eyes? As he thinks about it, he feels as if he's talking about someone other than himself. As Félix predicted, none of the Dolphins take part. *Stout fellows. True friends.* The rebels among the Toulouse swimmers are suspended. The president of the club, Guillaume Le Bras, is barred for life. During the two days of competition, Paule and Alfred don't leave their flat. Two days entirely devoted to their daughter Annie. Alone in the world.

★ ★ ★

The following week, Aaron discreetly slips a piece of paper into Alfred's pocket at the gym. Alfred unfolds it in the back room where he stores equipment. It's a press release from Fraternité, the liaison body of the 'French forces against racist barbarism'. He reads it several times. He's moved by this support and also reassured by the fighting spirit spreading in the shadows.

Do you know Nakache? Of course you do, everyone knows him. He's the French champion at 100 and 200 metres freestyle and the record holder for the 200 metres breaststroke. He has done more for the prestige of France and French youth sport than Pascot[32] and his ilk. But, because there is a but, Nakache is a French Jew. What a nerve on the part of a Jew to swim faster than a [. . .] Cartonnet [. . .] or any other militia man . . .

[. . .] He was also banned from participating in the most recent swimming competition. But they don't know the sports fans of Toulouse, and especially the swimmers of the Toulouse Olympic Employees Club (TOEC) and the Toulouse Athletic Club (TAC). The latter, outraged by this idiotic racist measure, have shown solidarity with Nakache and refused to take part in the championships, despite the threats of Pascot, the Chief Commissioner for Sports. [. . .] For a good ten minutes the stands rang with shouts of 'NAKACHE!' Thus the true sport-lovers of Toulouse showed their disgust for those who, by sabotaging sports, make themselves the protagonists of Teutonic methods.

'You're not alone, Alfred,' whispers Aaron, putting a hand on his shoulder.

Nevertheless, one by one the sports papers surrender to

the censorship of Vichy and the Gestapo, brutally reducing Nakache to anonymity and silence. Nothing is said about the reasons for his absence from competition. He no longer exists, or exists only on the pages of the innumerable anti-semitic journals. In its edition of 23 August, *Au pilori* gets vulgar: 'The Jew Nakache, the brilliant representative of French swimming, has not taken part in the French championships. Because he's injured. Where's the injury? On the foreskin? An unlucky snip of the shears?'

Auschwitz – Infirmary

Silhouetted in the semi-darkness of the infirmary entrance, Alfred sees Willy Holt, the young painter dedicated to gratifying the sometimes outrageous whims of the SS officers. His face is contorted with pain. For several days he has been struggling with a pus-filled abscess on his left ankle, the result of forced marches in wooden clogs, which is getting worse and worse.

'They've given me these three ointments for you,' sighs Alfred. 'I can't tell you which one to choose . . .'

'Pretty colours,' says Willy, gritting his teeth. 'Whitish-grey, delicate pink, sulphur yellow. Well, let's start with the pink one.'

Alfred applies the cream to the swelling deforming Willy's foot. He massages the ankle delicately while Willy clenches his fists.

'Well, how's it going in Kommando 78?' Alfred whispers,

to take Willy's mind off the burning sensations going all the way up to his knee.

'The cushiest of jobs, right after the kitchens,' he replies sarcastically. 'There are a dozen of us artists, led by a Polish kapo, Tadek, who's a painter himself and relatively kind. He's from Lodz, where he's left his wife and his little daughter behind. He often tells me about them, and gets very emotional.'

Alfred feels a pang of anguish at these words. Willy has forgotten that everything reminds Alfred of Annie.

'And what are you painting for them?' continues Alfred, to dispel the effect of this unintended blow.

'If you ignore the fantasies some of them have, it's mainly family portraits. I'm not saying it's gratifying work, but it's actually worthwhile. The fees are often food-based: bread, Polish pancakes, sometimes sugar. Most often cigarettes, as that's the easiest exchange to conceal.'

'Do you smoke?'

'I've never smoked. I can assure you that the sight of damage caused by tobacco doesn't encourage me to do so. So I swap the cigarettes for food. That allows me to aid those suffering from malnutrition, or otherwise I can help out the smokers with serious withdrawal symptoms who are at risk of going under.'

'Has it come to that?' asks Alfred, this time spreading the sulphur yellow ointment on Willy's swollen flesh.

'You can't imagine what it's like. The other day, out of curiosity, I went over to a group of six detainees crouching in a circle. They'd got together to take turns smoking a cigarette. Suddenly I saw a murderous look appear in some of their eyes.'

'Murder?'

'Yes, murder. If one of them draws on that cigarette too hard for too long, the worst could happen.'

'Men ready to kill for a puff of tobacco, that's the stage we've got to,' says Alfred sadly.

★ ★ ★

A few days later, Willy returns to the infirmary, walking more briskly.

'Well, how's that abscess?' asks Alfred, seeing him come in. 'It looks to me as if it's on the right track.'

'It definitely is, but I'm not sure it's thanks to your magic powder.'

Then, close to Alfred's ear: 'Find me something for headaches. My head's spinning. I can't do more than two brush strokes at a time and Tadek's backer wants his paintings.'

Alfred disappears, has a discreet chat with Professor Waitz, who rummages in a drawer and wraps some tablets in a handkerchief. All that's left to do is to slip this into Willy's hand. As he performs his sleight of hand trick, Alfred resumes the conversation in a mundane tone.

'And what does he want this time?'

'Some paintings to illustrate books of fairy-tales for his children.'

'Have you started?'

'Yes, and it's strange, it makes me relive happy days I thought I'd forgotten – gardens, beaches, games, forests, dogs, flowers, vegetable plots. The contrast with what we're going through here sparks my imagination.'

'How's that?'

'It's as if the pencils and brushes were moving almost by themselves into a graphic poetry that I'm not capable of.'

'And does he like it?'

'His children love it.'

Alfred remains silent, his eyes suddenly elsewhere. *Will this happy father give a thought to all those he has seen die howling with fear?*

Toulouse, 20 December 1943

Early one morning, there's a brutal knock at the door.

'Police, open up!'

Alfred pulls on a dressing gown and heads towards the front door of the flat.

'What do you want with me?'

'Open up or we'll break the door down!'

Paule has gone to be with Annie who has started to cry, terrified by the noise. He's hardly turned the handle when a dozen men in black push him roughly out of the way and disappear off into all the rooms.

'Alfred Nakache, you're under arrest, by order of the Gestapo. We're taking you to headquarters.'

'What about my wife and daughter?'

'They're coming with you. Take just a few clothes with you, nothing else, that'll be enough.'

They get ready quickly, piling a few things into a small suitcase. Without even thinking, Alfred removes two photos from their frames and slips them into his jacket pocket. The first one is of his entire family posing proudly at the edge of the Sidi M'Cid swimming pool. The second is a portrait of Annie on her first birthday. At Gestapo headquarters, they are made to sit in the foyer on the ground floor. Their arrival goes unnoticed. Gestapo officers are chatting with members of the Militia amid clouds of blue smoke. Secretaries laden with files go up and down the stairs in clattering heels. It's hot in this building, very hot. Unless that's their bodies reacting and trying to adapt to this cataclysm.

At least an hour passes before an elegant French civil servant politely asks Alfred to follow him upstairs. The head of the Gestapo himself, SS Karl Heinz Müller, wants to see him.

'Monsieur Nakache!' he yells, as Alfred enters his office. 'What a pleasure to meet you!'

He comes forward as though to shake his hand, but stops dead, eyeing him up and down.

'I thought you'd be taller, my friend, and burlier too, as a world record swimmer.'

His sarcasm leaves Alfred stonily indifferent. He doesn't answer.

'Keep in mind that I know your career like the back of my hand,' Müller adds, helping himself to a cup of coffee. 'What's more, I believe that your team beat ours at the Olympic Games in Berlin, in front of our beloved Führer.

That's not very nice, Monsieur Nakache. Nor are your little secret meetings with the Jewish Army in the beautiful countryside around Toulouse.'

The Jewish Army . . . Two words that, coming from Müller's pursed lips, condemn Alfred to death. His body stiffens.

'Relax, Alfred. You'll have plenty of time to think over your exploits when you're in the Saint-Michel prison, waiting for the long journey. Take him away!'

With his hands cuffed behind his back, Alfred walks back past Paule and Annie. His head is bent under the pressure of the paw of a soldier, who is crushing his neck. He hears Paule's voice, she's trying to say something to him, but her words are lost in the hubbub of the foyer. As he walks out through the door, her scream goes straight through him.

★★★

In Saint-Michel prison, an enormous, fortress-like building, one of the warders, Rodolphe Debrand, recognizes Alfred immediately. He worked at the TOEC swimming club for a while, as a caretaker. As they walk, he confirms that Paule is in detention in the women's wing.

'What about Annie?'

Rodolphe hesitates, ill at ease.

'The last I heard, she's been placed in the home for single mothers in the Rue Sainte-Lucie. She's safe.'

Annie snatched from her mother. From her parents. They'll stop at nothing. Rodolphe comforts Alfred as best he can, under the suspicious eye of his superior who is staring at them from the other side of the yard, playing with his keys.

'I have friends in town who will keep a watchful eye on her, Alfred, don't worry. And Minville has stopped by, so I'm told. He bought a stuffed toy for your daughter.'

Alfred smiles sadly. He tries not to let himself be overcome by emotion.

'And what have the papers been saying?'

'I don't know, Alfred.'

'Nothing, presumably?'

'I don't know. It doesn't matter.'

'So, nothing, then.'[33]

'We'll deal with it, don't worry.'

'Promise me you'll look after Paule. Tell her to be strong.'

Alfred shares a cell with Alain, a young member of the resistance network FTP-MOI.[34] This lad alone is a bastion against despair. He can't be more than about twenty years old. He has long, slicked-back fair hair and a hollow, angular face, but there are dark circles under his very pale blue eyes, and they look bloodshot. He looks insolently relaxed, but it's immediately obvious that he's suffered. He's heard of Nakache, of course, but he says he's not very interested in sport. It's not important. He's been studying literature in

Toulouse. 'Luckily I have books to take my mind off things. At least the ones we're allowed.'

Alfred is worried by what Alain tells him about the fate in store for the Jews. He talks about the internment camp in Drancy, north-east of Paris, and the convoys sent to Auschwitz in Poland, where many perish.

'We've got to get you out of here,' says Alain, 'but the Boches are all over the region, it's getting more and more difficult.'

Alain has few illusions about what awaits him. He's accused of terrorism, for throwing a grenade at a passing SS convoy. His leader, Marcel Langer, was guillotined in the yard in July, as were several of his comrades: Conchita, Maurice, Sylvain, Angèle, Raymond, Alice.

'Amid this heap of ruins,' Alain says with a smile, 'you have to keep your hopes up. Do you know the great writer André Malraux? Exactly ten years ago he won the Prix Goncourt for an amazing book, *La Condition humaine* [Man's Fate].'

'I don't read much, apart from swimming manuals.'

'This book is about how a group of communist revolutionaries planned the uprising in Shanghai in 1927. And it tells us that awareness of the absurd can co-exist with the certainty of being able to triumph over one's fate . . .'

'How?'

'By engaging with history, Alfred.'

'And did he apply it to himself?'

Alain's eyes light up with a hint of malice.

'Oh, yes! This famous intellectual is also a fierce resistance activist. He fought with the Maquis in the Lot before being arrested and imprisoned here. But they didn't reckon with the Angel brothers. The two of them didn't hesitate to use force. The day before Malraux was due to be transferred to Germany, they got him out of prison. Don't forget this story, Alfred, it will bring you luck.'

In his turn, Alain asks Alfred to talk about himself. The swimmer shows him the photo of his family, his parents and his two brothers. And the one of Annie that the warders had permitted him to keep. On that winter night, his first behind bars, Alfred takes his cellmate on a long journey to Constantine.

The silence of Forain

In his cell in the Saint-Michel prison, François Verdier learns to his amazement that the great champion Alfred Nakache, the Dolphin of Toulouse, was apprehended along with his wife and daughter only a few days after his own arrest. He has admired Artem in the pool, loudly applauding his exploits. The owner of an agricultural machinery business, a judge of the Toulouse commercial court and a great sports fan, Verdier is the leader of the biggest resistance network in the Haute-Garonne region. But Alfred is unaware of this. Nor does he know Verdier's codename, which is Forain [funfair].

On the morning of 13 December 1943, Verdier was arrested along with a hundred or so members of the Resistance. For this operation, codenamed 'Midnight', units of the SS and the Feldgendarmes, the German military police, assisted the Gestapo and its auxiliaries. A devastating raid for the Resistance. But on this day, imprisoned within four walls, Forain is thinking only of Nakache, furious that one of the stars of French sport is being attacked. Physically, Forain projects an image of honesty and impressive strength – impeccable head carriage and a deep-black gaze – that has not been altered by the violence of the blows to the face he has received. He gets hold of a pen and decides to get a secret message passed to Alfred.

It was Alain, the young member of the FTP-MOI resistance network with whom Nakache shared his cell, who took delivery of the message rolled up in a ball.

'Here, read this, it's for you, I'll explain . . .'

Alfred sits on the bench and carefully unfolds the sheet of paper:

Dear Alfred,

I was in the stands last year when you shattered the European record for the 100 metres butterfly. I had never seen such power in action. I was particularly dazzled by your smile as you got out of the pool. I often remember it when the days get sad. I'm disgusted by your being sidelined and now this arrest. You will certainly hear more about me in the coming days – I don't have enough space to write it here and in any case, it would be unwise – but be assured that I will try to do everything I can to get you out of here. Take care of yourself, champ.

Verdier

'I know Verdier, he's been to the gym several times,' says Alfred in surprise. 'He had a little word of encouragement for me each time. Why is he here?'

In a low voice, Alain confides: 'He's the head of the MUR, the United Resistance Movements for the Toulouse sector. Appointed directly by de Gaulle. An exceptional guy. He alone coordinates all the activities of the MUR: receiving parachute drops, planning sabotage, retrieving equipment, informing and contacting the Allies, recruitment, people smuggling, everyday management of underground members of the resistance, all under cover of selling of mowers, combine harvesters and Japy motors.'

'Does he take big risks?'

'I know only one thing, Alfred: he won't talk.'

April 1944 – Sport Libre

In Paris, Émile moves heaven and earth to get news of his friend. He does the rounds of the swimming clubs in the hope of picking up some news. No joy. Then he has the idea of contacting former pupils of the Janson-de-Sailly school. Good move: one of them advises him to get in touch with Raoul Gattegno, the leader of the Sport Libre network that was founded by the communists of the FGST, the Fédération Sportive et Gymnique du Travail.

In its pamphlets, Sport Libre denounces at length the measures against Jews and the enforced Aryanization of French sport. Raoul, a Jew with roots in Salonica, is in charge of the clandestine printing presses of the Young Communists. An excellent basketball player, he eludes the ever-tighter Gestapo checks thanks to a passport generously granted by the Spanish consulate. The friend with whom he set up Sport Libre, Auguste Delaune, has been killed. He was arrested by the French police on 27 July 1943 and died two months later as a result of the torture he suffered.

Despite this extreme pressure, Raoul manages to appear calm, the best kind of protection. He's arranged to meet Émile on a bench on the platform at Ivry-sur-Seine station, like two ordinary passengers waiting for the next train. He has news for him.

'Here, this is for you,' says Raoul with a smile, handing Émile a deluxe edition of the *Maxims* of La Rochefoucauld.

'You shouldn't have . . .'

'I think you'll like it.'

Émile opens the book and, to his amazement, finds that it contains the *Cahiers du Bolchévisme,* the journal of the French communist party.

'A very useful bit of sleight of hand in these difficult times,' sighs Raoul.

'What's your biggest problem today?' asks Émile.

'Paper. More and more difficult to find.'

'We're short of wheat. The family-run mill is more or less at a standstill.'

Raoul glances at the travellers crowded on the platform. Then he says quietly: 'So you're a friend of our swimming champion?'

'He's like a brother to me. All I know is that he's been carted off somewhere.'

'What I have to tell you isn't reassuring. We've put together a leaflet that will be mimeographed tomorrow.'

Raoul pulls a sheet of paper out of his jacket and slips it into Émile's hand. What he reads makes his blood run cold.

NAKACHE AND YOUNG PEREZ ARE IN SILESIA!!!

Following their plan to annihilate the French race, the Boches are taking on the best champions France has.

NAKACHE, the best swimmer in Europe, was recently arrested by the occupation authorities, along with his wife and his little daughter. All three have been taken to different locations. Nakache has been sent to the salt mines in Silesia, from which there is no return, and there he met YOUNG PEREZ, the little Tunisian boxer, who made the French colours shine particularly brightly by winning a world title. Young Perez now has tuberculosis and, by the will of the loathsome Boches, an athlete who was once envied, admired and respected by the crowds is no more than a human wreck and his days are numbered.

If the sportsmen of France do not take action, NAKACHE will suffer the same fate.

Action is crucial in order to rescue the prisoners and get them out of Hitler's gaols. Not to make the necessary effort to wrest the French champions from the clutches of the Boches would be unforgivable.

Stand up, sportsmen of France!!! Take action against the wreckers of French sport and youth. In all areas, tirelessly keep up the chant: NAKACHE, YOUNG PEREZ, MATTLER.

Let the Boches and their servants, the SS militiamen/ Cartonnet, Gibel [. . .] feel the vengeful rage of the sportsmen of France [. . .].

Drum up support at the stadiums and swimming pools.

Boo those who have sold out your sport to the enemies of the Fatherland.

Explain to those around you, to your friends, how those who are currently in power are destroying sport to satisfy their masters.

Join SPORT LIBRE in fighting against this rabble and preparing the ground to make sport truly free after the war, in order to provide our country with young people who are strong and happy to be alive.

– Sport Libre –

(Member of the United Forces of Patriotic Youth)

Alfred in Silesia, deep in the salt mines. With Perez and Mattler, the former captain of the French national football team. Émile's face starts to twitch and he struggles to control it. A memory of Mattler comes back to him in a flash. In December 1938, Mattler had caused a sensation after the revenge match between Italy and France in Naples. In an inn filled with Italian football fans, he had climbed on a table and, standing ramrod straight, had sung the *Marseillaise,* despite the defeat. This act of bravery had been applauded in most of the newspapers. In the Sport Libre leaflet, Nakache's rival Jacques Cartonnet is targeted by name. Émile had always distrusted him. When he points at Cartonnet's name on the paper with a questioning look, Raoul replies by raising his eyebrows in a way that suggests there will be difficult days ahead for the swimmer turned militiaman.

'What about Paule and Annie? Where are they?' asks Émile.

'I don't know anything more about them. If there is any news, I'll pass it on to you.'

Raoul stands up abruptly. Without another look at Émile, he gets on the train that has just pulled in at the station.

July 1944 – Arms stretched out in the shape of a cross

Aiding the weakest of the detainees helps Alfred to bear his own suffering. To forget he's had no news of his family, to wipe from his consciousness what is evidently clear: that the Auschwitz camp is a killing factory. Its gas chambers and cremation furnaces are, as everyone now knows, the deadly cogs of an extermination machine.

How could the German people have spawned such a monstrosity? How could France have thrown him onto a train with Paule and Annie and delivered them into the hands of these barbarians? Just yesterday, when he and Professor Waitz were on their way to see an SS man with lung disease, they passed a mound resembling a slag heap that they should never have seen: a heap of compacted corpses, bristling in places with ossified arms and legs, like twisted steel rods sticking out of a block of concrete. With every passing month, the smell of death impregnates their clothing more and more.

Bathing in the water tanks at the other end of the camp becomes a necessity. Vital, physical and mental purification. Last Saturday at nightfall, they had another race, with Noah swimming freestyle and Artem breaststroke. The star of the pool tied his legs together with an elastic band to give himself a handicap. In this thick, dirty water, Alfred won by a short head. Although he's grown thinner and his muscles are like jelly, he still has speed. That's something. The Dolphin isn't completely washed up on the banks of horror yet.

After the race, floating on their backs with their arms stretched out in the shape of a cross, the two swimmers idle in the middle of the pool for a long time. Like two pieces of driftwood. Charles, the last lookout posted at the back of the pool, gives them a sign. They've got plenty of time. No movement of boots in the sleeping camp. Alfred has complete confidence in Charles. Whenever he can, he takes a few sheets of paper from the infirmary so that this Art Déco fan can work on his designs for blocks of flats. The lad has two obsessions: roof-terraces and bay windows.

Relaxed, with his body half submerged, Alfred talks to Noah about Algeria again. *Why*, he wonders, *does childhood keep coming back to me?* He tells him about the Philippeville Christmas Cup, the race held in the Bay of Skikda that made him into one of the great hopes of swimming, describes to him the astonishing beauty of this shoreline where rocks emerge from the clear water like a string of beads. And in the middle, poised on top of a mountainous island, a huge white lighthouse. How often he has dreamed of it during his restless nights, this majestic lighthouse keeping watch over a world that has now been submerged, with memories as the last mooring ropes.

'Have I already told you about my grandmother Sarah?'

'Never.'

'Selfless. Generosity incarnate. She spends her days in the family kitchen in Kar Chara concocting little dishes. In the evenings, she dozes off exhausted on her low chair. Her little kitchen smells of warm bread, mint and coriander. She's the world champion of a kind of lemon we call créponné. It's an institution in Constantine – in summer, all the young people gather in the Rue Caraman and the Place de la Brèche to treat themselves to a créponné. My grandmother makes it herself. Would you like to know her recipe?'

'It's already making me drool.'

'First, she makes sugar syrup with freshly squeezed lemon juice and pours it into the drum of the ice-cream maker, an old round wooden sorbetière. Then she fills the container with crushed ice that's been smashed with a hammer. She adds coarse salt and then she churns and churns, she churns hard enough to break her arms, until the lemon-flavoured liquid freezes and turns frothy. A real treat.'

'You love your grandmother . . .'

Alfred replies with a melancholy smile that twists his face. Then he regains his childlike expression: 'I always used to watch her peel and slice or dice the vegetables and the lemons at fantastic speed, like a magician. Her eyesight was failing and her body weak, but her hands were surprisingly agile.'[35]

While Léon, Gérard and Charles keep watch, Noah shows Alfred the sky spangled with stars. Auriga, the Orion nebula, the cluster of the Pleiades, he knows them all. In this necklace of golden stars, Alfred believes he can make out Paule's eyes. 'A wink from the great creator,' jokes Noah as he starts turning a backwards somersault in the water.

A whistle. First one, then another. The alerts mimic the song of a tit. The sound of approaching boots. Get out of the water as quickly as possible, pull on pyjamas over wet skin. Go back up to the barracks following the route indicated by the lookouts. Overcome fear. Remain men. For seven Sundays in a row over the summer, Alfred and Noah brave the Nazis to enjoy these moments of eternity. Until the wintry weather of November and the return of the great cold.

October 1944, *L'Écho d'Alger*, a daily newspaper in Algiers:

THE CHAMPION NAKACHE IS DEAD, A VICTIM OF
THE BOCHES IN SILESIA

Algiers. – The newspaper *Le Patriote de Lyon* reports, under the byline of Monsieur Henri Berne, the following information on the death of the French swimming champion and world record holder Nakache in a concentration camp: 'We will no longer see this great figure of French swimming in the pool. We will not see our champion again. His physical strength was equalled only by his personal ethics: "Artem" died a victim of the Boches because he was Jewish.'

We know that the C.G. [the General Commissioner for Sport] forced him to withdraw from the French championships in Toulouse. In the face of this injustice, his fellow sportsmen spontaneously refused to participate in the competition, which enraged his enemies, who did not hesitate to have him arrested by the Nazis. Nakache was taken to Drancy, the antechamber of death, with his wife and child. He was then transferred to a salt mine in Silesia. The sad news comes from there.

So the only world record holder we had was killed by the Boches. Nakache was born in Constantine on 18 November 1915. He died at the height of his powers, at the age of 29, when he could still have achieved numerous great feats.

Christmas 1944 – Auschwitz

Léon the electrician no longer has the heart to sing. Goodbye to the songs of Charles Trenet. No more joy. No more swallows in the sky, only the enormous ravens that swirl around in the blinding light of the camp's searchlights. Ever since his arrival, this sight has caused an apocalyptic vision in Léon. He doesn't sing any more. He reports the unthinkable to Alfred, Gérard and Victor Perez, and also to Kid Marcel, another boxer who's a bit of a thug, emaciated by Auschwitz. He tells all of them that yesterday, on Christmas Eve, in the middle of the night, he and his friends from the electricians' squad were woken up by a detachment of the SS.[36]

'The officer yelled *"Alles schnell raus!"* Get out!' begins Léon, in a toneless voice. 'A few metres from the block there was a lorry waiting for us. With Monsieur Morzan – *why does everyone address that fellow as monsieur? Because he immediately inspires respect, that's just how it is* – we decided that if it was going to Birkenau and the crematorium, the best thing to do would be to capture an SS man as we're getting out of the lorry, any one of them will do, and wring his neck. We'd die, but so would he.'

'Quite right!' says Kid Marcel.

'During the drive, the tarpaulin cover meant we couldn't work out where we were going. There wasn't a smell of gas, that was a good sign. The lorry stopped. The kapos told us to jump out. We were in a snow-covered field. It must have been 3 o'clock in the morning. Devilishly cold. In front of us, a bit further away, was a railway track with a railway wagon on it. Not a train, just a railway wagon on its own. The SS told the kapos that we were to go over to the wagon, open it up and put everything we found there into the lorry. I don't remember who opened the door. Inside . . . babies. Nothing but babies. Very young infants who all looked dead, whether they were clothed or naked. The smell wasn't good.'

'Stop, Léon,' says Perez.

'No, go on,' Alfred interrupts, thinking that Léon needs to talk.

'So we had to get out the babies and take them to the lorry. The SS told us we had to stow them neatly because the two vehicles didn't hold the same amount. There were many more in the wagon than would fit into the lorry. We climbed in, took a baby, jumped down, went over to the lorry which was ten metres away and neatly stowed the dead baby in it. We did it five, ten, twenty times. The pile in the lorry was beginning to grow. We continued the return trips. At one point, Morzan was in one line, I was in the other, and we passed one another. And when we met, Morzan was standing in the middle, petrified, with a baby in his arms. I said: "Wait, Monsieur Morzan, what's going on?" He replied: "Léon, the baby isn't dead." Then I left my line and said to him: "Come with me, we'll tell the SS. We'll be braver together, the two of us." We went up to one of the SS men and Morzan, jabbering in broken German, explained that the baby wasn't dead and was still moving. The SS man looked at us like we were a couple of idiots. He had the solution. He took the poor baby from Morzan's arms by its feet. He went like this . . . and wham, he slammed it against the frame of the lorry. The baby fell to the ground.'

'That's enough, Léon,' sighs Alfred, taking him by the shoulder.

But the electrician wants to finish.

'The SS man got out a revolver, took aim at the child and fired. He looked at us with a big smile and said: "*Kind kaputt,* you see how easy the solution is: the child is dead." Morzan picked up the poor baby and we carried it to the lorry. When the wagon was empty, the lorry drove off and the twenty SS men took us back to the block.'

Léon catches his breath.

'It was already daylight. That was my Christmas Eve, folks.'

Evacuation

And what's happening in the world beyond the watchtowers during this time? Scraps of news reach them, overheard snatches of conversations between officers. Like Noah, Robert Waitz, who's from Strasbourg, speaks German fluently. He understands that the Soviet troops are making rapid progress, and that the Third Reich, so sure of its supremacy, is cracking everywhere, under attack on the other front by the American landings.

The noose is tightening, and it's even rumoured that Hitler is cornered.

'We have to hold on, Alfred,' whispers Robert, with fatherly affection.

In fact, at the start of 1945, the camp staff seem to be overcome by panic. Military lorries filled with trunks drive past distraught detainees, left to their own devices. Stalin's troops are said to be only a few kilometres away and sufficient reinforcements are not expected from Germany.

On 18 January 1945, evacuation is ordered. The soldiers are racing around. What are they going to do with the detainees? Rather than just leaving them there and hurrying off back to Germany, they round up the fittest and make them line up in columns, yelling like madmen, abandoning the elderly and sick or mowing them down in a hail of machine-gun fire.

It's the start of the death march.

Little soldier

Freezing cold, minus ten degrees Celsius, dogs barking, SS men striking the stragglers, sometimes the sharp sound of a shot echoing across the plain, there are thousands of them moving past a forest, in a formation of twenty columns, five men across, starving and thirsty, not knowing where they're going. Hell isn't behind them. It too has left the barracks of Auschwitz to accompany them towards a new abyss. It won't let go of them, biting their tortured bodies until they bleed.

Alfred marches alongside Noah, his mate from the pool. Has he become a friend? He's no longer quite sure what friendship means. *A partner, yes, a loyal, trustworthy companion.* Victor Perez, the boxer, has joined them too. Victor is still brave, even though he bears the scars of his imprisonment. He's emaciated and has lost nearly all his teeth. He continued to put on the gloves to outwit the Nazi officers. Tragi-comic fights. Show fights. Pathetic passports to win the right to live.

Like Alfred and Noah, Perez helps the weakest to get back up. In unreal bursts of energy, he tells funny stories, using mockery as a crutch. He pretends to connive with the soldiers surrounding them, some of them very young, maybe fifteen or sixteen, whose fear can be read on their childlike faces. Rations are short, even for them. It's a flight, a rout, an aimless march. *With no border between day and night.* When the SS have had enough, they stop the column. Then they regroup, huddling together to try to keep warm and get some sleep. Alfred has got into the habit of settling down against Victor's back, curled up like a foetus.

'How long will we be able to keep going, Victor?'

He breathes heavily and doesn't reply immediately. 'In the ring, Artem, the fight is never lost,' he whispers. 'One round can change everything. It's the same in the pool. An attack of cramp, a mouthful of water swallowed, and your opponent is trailing. Nothing's written in stone.'

'You remind me of Alban, my coach in Toulouse, always optimistic before a competition.'

'Monte-Cristo, my friend, don't forget Monte-Cristo.'

'I don't even know what's become of Paule and Annie. Last night I dreamed they'd gone back to Constantine.'

'You'll find them, Artem. Try to sleep.'

That evening, Alfred was able to close his eyes for about an hour. Victor slept for longer. Alfred admires his mentality, his strength of mind. The heart of a boxer still beats inside his emaciated body. The days pass and the landscape is unchanging. Dead trees creaking in the wind, icy paths, snow-covered plains darkened by a low, grey sky. And the gnawing hunger. Men fall and don't get up again. Usually they're finished off with a bullet in the head.

But there's also this young one SS boy, the last recruit of a crumbling empire, whom Alfred sees going discreetly over to a silhouette on the ground. The poor man has his hand stretched heavenward. The soldier places a piece of bread in his palm. One by one he closes the frozen fingers over the slice, so it doesn't end up in the snow. He also says a few words to him that Alfred can't hear, then runs back to his patrol. His superiors haven't noticed. Trembling, the man on the ground puts the bread in his mouth. Alfred and Noah help him to get up. To resume the mechanical march of his unconscious body. *Who is this kid in uniform? The SS outfit doesn't suit him very well*. He turns round to check that the man is on his feet again, that he's moving forward. The little soldier smiles and shakes his head. In the chaos of this Dantesque march, his gesture is a light in the darkness.

Not that, Victor . . .

Now it's snow that they stuff into their stony mouths. Snow to allay the thirst that devours them. Ladles of water are no longer being circulated, there's not a drop to put on their tongues. The complaints turn into unbearable groans. It sounds like the harsh scraping of a broken violin, or a saw cutting them up one after the other. When the column has stopped to allow the soldiers to refuel, Young Perez makes a sign to Alfred. Behind the high embankment, at the far end of a clearing, he has spotted smoke from a chimney.

'What do you want to do?'

'Search for grub, Alfred.'

'Are you crazy?'

'What about Edmond Dantès, what do you think he did? The Boches are far enough away. It's our last chance.'

Alfred doesn't have time to persuade him not to do something so stupid. Victor leaves the column, climbs over the mound and disappears among the trees. Alfred tries to locate him, but there's no sign of him, just a curtain of leafless bushes and the shadow of a house. Interminable minutes pass. Alfred is afraid a soldier will come towards them and notice Victor's absence. He's well known, a star who attracts attention. And then he reappears, his arms laden with two bags of food. Beaming, he yells: 'There'll be enough for everyone!' At the same moment, an SS man comes out of the wood, adjusting his flies after having a pee. He turns towards Victor. The boxer drops his bags. Then, without taking his eyes off his friends, he collapses under a hail of bullets from a submachine gun.

The SS shout at them to get back into columns of five, hitting them with sticks to make them regroup more quickly. Alfred is caught up in this cluster of terrorized men. He has lost sight of Victor. He would like to die too. The sky is filled with clouds in end of the world colours.

★ ★ ★

After a march of seventy kilometres, the SS divide the columns in two outside the Gleiwitz camp. Why? To go where? The officers refuse to explain. But a rumour runs through the ranks of this troop of living dead. Some will leave for Dora and others, like Alfred, will go to Germany. Fate is definitely not on his side. In the middle of this no man's land, he and Noah have to say goodbye. Alfred embraces him tightly.

'You have dazzled me, my boy. Make something of your life.'

'I promise,' he smiles. 'I won't soon forget the swimmer of Auschwitz.'

★ ★ ★

Under truncheon blows, they are pushed into roofless metal railway wagons, open to the sky. Without food, crammed together like animals for three days. Like all those months ago when they left Drancy. Except that this time, Alfred is on his own. Without Paule or Annie, of whom he has no news. Annie who's another year older, who must be talking by now, dancing, singing, cheerful like her mother. At each stop on their journey, villagers throw them pieces of bread, in order to watch, doubled up with laughter, the desperate fights resulting from their generosity.

Alfred struggles against hunger and thirst and also, like all his companions in misfortune, against the icy cold that seeps in everywhere. The noise of the wagons on the tracks is unbearable. They're like disjointed dolls swaying from right to left and front to back. He has a splitting migraine. Beside him a man who's no longer young holds his hand. Tears are pouring down his face. He doesn't know where he's going either. Nor has he had any news of his family. The dead are pushed overboard to make space. As at Auschwitz, there's a violent halt. The train wheels squeal and then sigh. Then silence. *Snow, smoke, dizziness* . . . So this is it, the end of the road. Outside this immense fortress, set on top of the Ettersberg hill and exposed to the north wind. Buchenwald, in Germany.

A new interment.

A new number: 122441.

As at Auschwitz, everyone is ordered to undress. Their bodies are frozen, starving, covered with lice. Some are sick with typhus. In front of them is a large pool filled with black water.

'Get in there and cross it with your heads underwater!' yell the SS.

Alfred has spotted Léon. The street urchin is frightened, trembling all over. The SS speed things up with blows from their truncheons. Alfred helps Léon to climb down the metal ladder. He holds his hand as they slowly go down into the murky water that comes up higher than their necks when they reach the bottom.

'Take a good deep breath,' Alfred whispers to him, 'and walk forward steadily, holding your breath. It's a matter of ten metres, no more. I'll be right behind you.'

Léon nods with the rigid look of someone entrusting his life to a friend. Around them, men are struggling and drowning without a word. Alfred and Léon move forward slowly and reach the other side. Alfred gathers his strength to give Léon a sharp push up onto the ladder. At the top, on the paving surrounding the pool, detainees armed with fire hoses are waiting for them. They spray them down with incredible violence to remove the sticky paste covering their tired bodies. *Disinfectant, they dunked us in Cresyl, a toilet disinfectant*, thinks Alfred, who fears the consequences for those who swallowed any of it.

In this sinister, overpopulated camp – every day, hundreds of evacuees arrive from all over the place and are added to the detainees already there – the Nazi officers carry out the selection process. A kapo goes up to Léon: '172749, that's you, isn't it? You're an *elektriker*? OK, you're the one I'm looking for.'

Alfred pricks up his ears: 'What's he saying?'

'About a hundred kilometres from here, in a town called Sonneberg, there's an important factory that makes gears. They're short of electricians and engineers. The employment services for deportees have told them about the existence of our group of specialists from Monowitz.'

'That's a bit of luck for you, Léon. We'll see each other again . . .' The kapo brutally interrupts their goodbyes. Alfred is taken to the 'little camp', to the infirmary of the block for the sick and disabled. He has been recognized immediately by the superior officer in charge of the selection. Just like at Buna-Monowitz, the SS officer in charge looks pleased to have him in his ranks.

The name of the 'little camp' at Buchenwald is misleading. It's a huge place where people are left to die. Men can be seen just collapsing all of a sudden. Alfred is intrigued by a tall silhouette at the entrance to the barracks, shrouded in mist. The man is wearing a black beret and large rectangular glasses that cut across his oblong face. He's limping slightly. Alfred is sure he knows him. He goes over to him and recgonizes him immediately: Roger Foucher-Créteau, a journalist from Toulouse, a member of the resistance and the brother of André, one of the swimmers in the Dolphins team. He remembers that Roger had started a clandestine journal, *Les Légions françaises anti-Axe* (the French Legions against the Axis). When they used to bump into each other in the bistro, Roger never stopped condemning the dangers of Nazism.

'I've often thought about you,' sighs Alfred, embracing him. 'I even had a feeling that our paths would cross again one day. Do you believe me?'

'I've been here over a year,' replies Roger in a firm voice. 'I'd rather you told me about Auschwitz.'

'Indescribable loneliness. We French speakers helped one another as much as we could. I haven't had any news of my wife and daughter.'

Roger pauses for a few moments.

'No one could have imagined anything like that, Alfred, no one.'

'Not even you, despite all your warnings . . .'

In particular, none of us could have imagined this sword of Damocles hanging over our heads, Alfred says to himself. *A sword in the hands of Jacques Cartonnet, that despicable man who pretended to be our friend.*

With a wave of his hand, Roger motions for Alfred to step aside. Behind the building. He makes sure that no guards are watching them, then takes a big notebook out of his jacket.

'It's a memory book recording my thoughts, my drawings, and those of all my friends. If you'd like to write something in it one day, don't hesitate.'

He hands Alfred the forbidden book. If he's caught with it, he knows that he and all those who've written in it will be shot. Alfred leafs through it quickly.

'Take your time,' says Roger. 'Read some of the passages.'

Alfred comes across a page where Roger describes 'the slave market' that is organized every morning 'in the semi-darkness of a vague dawn'.

'I'll tell you later. Carry on.'

There, at the top left, is Marcel Michelin, from the family of industrialists, who notes: 'I'm fifty-eight, I know what it is to "drink up obstacles". He's fat, but we'll have him all the same.' Alfred smiles at this reference to the Michelin advertising slogan and the company's chubby mascot made out of tyres. This Marcel is a determined man.

On the next page, Armand Pesquier, an employee of the Toulouse prefecture, contents himself with two lines. His name is familiar to Alfred. He was a member of the resistance network Françoise.[37] But he's feeling gloomy: 'Everything I can write is meaningless, because my internment in Buchenwald has made me lifeless. I apologize.'

They all talk about the camp as a 'jungle' – a space that is both ruled by violence and anarchic, where life hangs by a thread. Alfred takes a last look at the book. A certain Dr Froger, a doctor from Indre-et-Loire, makes a strange recommendation: 'In Buchenwald more than anywhere else the Vedas are applicable.'

'What are the Vedas, Roger?'

'Philosophical Buddhist writings. Everything is useful in this pigsty.'

Balanced unsteadily on his injured leg, Roger takes back the book. He turns the pages, looking for a final word.

'Here, look at this, it's a poem by a German prisoner, Anton Zeimer, addressed to me. I've put the translation in the margin; I think it's faithful.'

Alfred reads the text slowly, with his head turned towards the wall.

I have sun in my heart, I have confidence and courage
I have sun in my heart and all will go well
And if, one day, my name comes into your mind
Think inside yourself that
you have known me.

Sun in one's heart. The image is as sweet as clear water. The Dolphin of Toulouse, the kid from Constantine, has the impression that this German is talking about him, about his little paradise of Sidi M'Cid, about life as he loved it. Who is he, and why is he in here? He won't forget these words. He'll even repeat them to himself every day to chase away the dark ideas and give himself courage. *Hope*, he says to himself, *will be the last thing to die.*

A month later, on 26 January, he asks Roger for his memory book. He has written a rough draft. It's the first time in fifteen months that he's held a pen. But that evening when the loudspeakers are broadcasting the songs of Zarah Leander, the Swedish muse of the Nazis, behind the thick curtain of snow, it's not sun but thunder that's in his heart. Alfred starts by briefly describing his reunion with Foucher-Créteau. Then he gets down to it:

> A day will come . . . the sufferings, the tortures, the ashes of the crematoriums call for justice, and then an inexorable vengeance will sweep down on these barbarians. We still have some hard times to go through, but full of resolution we will reach the new road that the new humanity will have traced for itself.

At the bottom of the page, Alfred, who isn't particularly religious, adds in French and Yiddish: *All was written and with God's will, we will get through it.*

11 April 1945

Their saviours have arrived. The Yanks. The GIs, their cousins, the guys of the 7th army. They look proud. Real cowboys, cigarettes in their mouths, helmets askew, sunglasses on their noses. Most of them are chewing gum. Wrigley's, the best. However, what they see on entering the camp turns their stomachs. They lower their eyes, cover their faces with handkerchiefs. Mounds of emaciated corpses, mountains of clothes and shoes. And then these ghostly beings wandering around blindly. Men and women without a compass, imprisoned in their madness. They should have been warned, but all the same. They learn to cope with it very quickly. As liberators, certain of their mission.

It's their relaxed attitude, even more than their efficiency, that leaves Alfred stunned. Army nurses offer their pretty arms to help him reach the field hospital. He refuses politely. He's fit enough to walk without help. He gives his particulars: Alfred Nakache, born 18 November 1915 in Constantine.

French of Algerian origin, Jew, top-level swimmer, teacher of physical education and sport. A wife, Paule, a child, Annie. Arrested in Toulouse on 20 December 1943. Deported to Auschwitz on 23 January 1944.

In the tent, the doctor, Colonel Colins, weighs him. A mere forty kilos, half his weight when he was in shape. Colins listens to his chest, palpates him, observes him. His lungs are a bit tired and he has skin infections here and there, because of malnourishment. His feet could also do with a bit of a rest. But nothing serious.

'You'll be able to get on the plane. Go back to France. Draw a line through all this,' he says in perfect French.

'Do you know France?'

'Oh yes, my friend! After the liberation of Paris, in August last year, I stayed there for some time. And I learned fast.'

He has a sparkle in his eye. Before Alfred disappears behind the canvas, he calls out to him: 'Hey! Nakache! Don't forget to go back to swimming. The Yankees are waiting for you any time.'

Alfred shrugs his shoulders as if to say, why not? *A nice guy, this Yank* . . .

Reconnecting with the world

28 April 1945. In his room at the Hôpital de la Pitié-Salpêtrière, lying on a freshly made bed, Alfred hears children playing down below. For the first time in months, he has slept deeply. As he opens his eyes, the echo of his dream is still with him, hazy and strange. He's playing water polo with his brothers in the Sidi M'Cid pool. Young Perez, Noah and Félix also seem to be there, fighting for the ball under a blazing sun.

Above then, perched on a high diving board that doesn't really exist, a kind of immaculately white Eiffel Tower, Paule is preparing to do a new dive. She's maybe thirty metres above them, her back to the pool, wearing a blue swimsuit with a low back that sparkles with a thousand stars. Her legs are long and golden. They stop their game to encourage her. She pushes off, arms stretched out behind her, curls up in a ball, but instead of plunging straight into the water, her rotations accelerate and turn into a furious whirlwind that makes her disappear in a white cloud.

While everyone is looking for her in the middle of the clouds, she starts playing hide and seek. From time to time, she sticks out her head – 'Here I am, boys!' – then disappears again. The nurse comes into the room, brusquely interrupting his dream.

'Someone's asking to see you.'

'Who is it?'

' A journalist who says he's a friend of yours.'

'Tell him to come in.'

Old Bernard! It's been years since he covered Alfred's competitions for French radio. A man from the Plaine de la Limagne, in the Auvergne, shrewd and friendly, whose father runs a bistro on the Rue Delhomme, in the Vaugirard district of Paris. Le Mont d'Or, that's its name. One of his favourite places. The best aligot in town.

'At least you haven't got thin, Bernard.'

'And you haven't lost your sense of humour, Alfred my boy.'

The Dolphin takes his hand and shakes it as hard as he can.

'What on earth are you doing here?'

'An ambulance man recognized you and tipped me off. Everyone here thinks you died a long time ago.'

Bernard hands him a cutting from *L'Écho d'Alger* dating from October 1944. It's a strange feeling to read the report of your own death. In his bag, Bernard also has an article that was published a month ago in Toulouse, in *La République*. It's entitled 'Those we will not forget' – in other words, those who have 'disappeared'. It covers Artem's performances, his 'sporting honesty', his 'seriousness'. Bernard tells Alfred that the new mayor of Toulouse has decided to name the new municipal swimming pool after him. He's had a plaque in memory of Alfred placed on one of the walls of the indoor pool and gathered together all the notables of the region for the inauguration.

'I'm going to announce your return, if you agree. At least things will be done properly.'

'You haven't lost your bearings, you crafty devil.'

For his scoop, Bernard asks him a few simple questions, one of which astounds him: 'Will you go back to swimming?' But Bernard doesn't look as if he's joking. There's even a great deal of affection in his eyes. Alfred reflects for a moment. He wonders if his journalist friend really understands what he's been through; if anyone has told him that he came back alone. Without Paule. Without Annie. The next day, Nakache sees his full answer in the papers: 'I've come back from my tomb. Let me get back in touch with the world of the living. After that, I'll try swimming again.'

★ ★ ★

It's with Émile, and no one else, that Alfred wants to leave Paris. Émile has come to pick him up from the hospital. Émile hasn't changed, a sprightly imp, always in a good mood.

The faithful friend who kept writing to him in Toulouse to encourage him. And to warn him. He looks so happy to see Alfred again, which he quickly admits he didn't believe would ever happen. There's a group of photographers standing outside the entrance. A few fans as well, waiting for an autograph. Alfred smiles, dazzled by the flashes. He signs the backs of yellowed photographs that seem to him to have come from a different age. They show him in swimming trunks, on the edge of a pool, always with that air of laughter.

Alfred takes time to talk to these people who haven't forgotten him. Some of them ask him what it was like there. Words fail him. He stammers 'hard, very hard' a few times, which doesn't tell them anything. A young woman tearfully explains that her entire family was arrested and taken to the Vélodrome d'Hiver in 1942, that she escaped thanks to their cleaner who hid her in her room on the sixth floor, that she had no news of anyone, that their names do not appear anywhere, neither on the lists of deportees posted at the Hôtel Lutetia, nor anywhere else.

Alfred would like to tell her that he hasn't had any news of Paule and Annie either. That he has learned that François Verdier was killed by the Boches. In spite of the torture and cruelty he suffered, Forain never revealed any secrets to the Gestapo. Witnesses saw him in a terrible physical state during his transfers between the Saint-Michel prison and the German police headquarters. On 27 January 1944, the

Gestapo secretly took him to the Forest of Bouconne, to the west of Toulouse. On an isolated path, his executioners killed him with a bullet to the abdomen. 'Perhaps in order to wipe out any traces of their barbarity', read Alfred in *Le Patriote du Sud-Ouest*, 'or, alternatively, in order to accentuate the degree of horror, the two Gestapo officers shattered the head of the resistance leader with a grenade placed in his mouth.'

Alfred would also like to tell her that he has no news of Aaron Stein, the man close to the Jewish Army who liked to use the punching bag at his gym. He was last seen in the spring of 1944, at the Médiéval, a café nestled at the foot of the towers of the Château de Foix, in Ariège. Nothing more since then. No news of either Léon the electrician or Gérard the Marseillais, those two friends from Drancy and Auschwitz. He would like to confide all the things that torment him to this woman to try to soothe hers. But nothing comes out. He wishes her a meaningless, disappointing 'good luck' and embraces her tenderly.

'Come on, old pal, you'll miss your train,' Émile says to tear him away from her.

★ ★ ★

Several times during the journey, as he's dozing off, the monotonous rumbling of the train reminds him of the deadly rhythm of convoy 66. Don't think about it, try to chase away these nightmare images by looking out of the window and contemplating the changing scenery of the beautiful French countryside. The green of Poitou, the hills of the Limousin, the arid limestone plateaux of the Lot Valley. God, how beautiful this country is, despite the scars of war.

As they arrive at each station, it's the same desolation: collapsed blocks of flats, roads torn open, towns battered and bleeding, trying to rise again. *What will my 'pink city' look like? Was it also bombed?* When he dozes off, he revisits Toulouse, street by street, stopping for a drink at the Bibent or the Petit Chalet, walking along the Garonne, opening the heavy door of the gym, well before the noise of boots and shouts, putting his things in the changing rooms of the pool that now bears his name.

His eyelids slowly close. He lets himself slide into his dreams. Soon he's on the block, his arms down, his head hunched in his shoulders. On your marks, get set . . .? The softness of the water against his skin gives him goose bumps. The sensation of speed takes over his whole body. The desire is there, intense, vibrant, intact, while the train speeds along its route. With his eyes shut, he regains contact with the living world. With his eyes shut, he starts to swim again.

Notebook

On the first day of training, Alban Minville is gracious enough to act as though nothing had happened. He stands at the edge of the pool, chain-smoking. And mimes, like the perfectionist he is, the perfect movements – for breaststroke, for butterfly. In the water, Alfred's muscles are quite weak. He doesn't pull too hard, in order to avoid tears.

'Reach, reach,' he repeats to himself, over and over.

Alfred empties his mind and, gradually, his senses take over. They carry him faster and faster to the other side of the pool. It seems that the dolphin Nakache isn't quite dead yet.

'It's even better than yesterday,' says Minville every evening, as if he's saying it for the first time.

His teammates, Alex Jany and Georges Vallerey, also seem to agree.

'It's the return of the three musketeers!' exclaims Alex, whose family has become a bit like Alfred's own.

'*Inchallah!*' thunders Georges.

Georges Vallerey is the youngest member of the club. Everyone calls him Yoyo. A force of nature and a fiery temperament who grew up in Casablanca, in Morocco. The youngest of a family of swimmers known as 'les Poissons', the fish, whose father had competed in the swimming events at the 1924 Olympic Games in Paris. Four years ago, on 8 November 1942, when he was only fifteen, Georges showed incredible courage.

On that day, the Americans, who were expected as liberators, bombed the port of Casablanca, where there were three French ships under the command of the Vichy regime, the *Primauguet*, the *Milan* and the *Albatros*. Dozens of sailors fell into the water. Some couldn't swim, others, weighed down by their equipment or wounded, were struggling to avoid drowning. Along with his friend Robert Guenet, who was aged twenty-nine, young Georges didn't hesitate. At the foot of the Black Rocks, he got undressed and, with bombs raining down, tossed about by the swell, he set off to help them. Covered in oil, his skin torn by the scrap metal floating on the water, Yoyo launched a little flat-bottomed boat that was lying on the pebbly beach into the water, in order to pick up as many of the shipwrecked sailors as he could. Ignoring the danger – 'like a game in which he uses all his skill and speed, without complaining and without a trace of tiredness'[38] – the boy rowed with all his might, making a series of round trips and saving a total of over fifty soldiers in an apocalyptic atmosphere. 'His prodigious courage amazes and inspires me,' said his friend Robert, who, for his part, was 'gritting [his] teeth to keep from screaming'.[39]

In the Dolphins team, Yoyo shows the same commitment. He never talks about the rescue. With Nakache, who is almost the same age as Robert was in the hell off Casablanca, he's the same little brother. Cheerful, willing, knowing no bounds. His joie de vivre brings a few smiles to Alfred's face but, like all the affection surrounding him, it never quite seems to manage to ease the sorrows that assail him.

★ ★ ★

However much Alfred succeeds in forgetting about Paule and Annie's absence when he's in the water, as soon as he gets out of the pool, he is haunted by their faces. Thanks to Jany senior, he is back in the flat they used to live in. Nothing is left of the furniture they had found in second-hand shops, apart from a clock from which the mechanism has been removed. As for the rest, the Gestapo and the Militia have taken everything. Books, medals and cups. The Janys have lent him a bed. The little food he eats is as well balanced as possible. Above all, it's important not to eat to excess. He takes care not to stuff himself. He doesn't feel the need for it. He has neither the strength to go to the bistro for a drink, nor any desire to go back to the gym. The man who now runs it is a former rugby player, like his predecessor, and it seems to be doing well. Alfred spends his evening alone, sitting at the table in front of the window that looks out onto the street. Sometimes he listens to one of Cheikh Raymond's records that a friend has found for him. The lyrics resonate with him. *Delicately, he approaches his beloved. His soul is torn apart.* He opens his post, checks the times of the trains from Paris. He copies them meticulously into a little purple notebook.

No question of missing an arrival. He'd rather skip a training session than miss their reunion. Almost every day, with a little rose hidden in the depths of his pocket, he walks to Matabiau station to welcome Paule and Annie. People look at him with embarrassment. He often stays on the platform for a long time. Stranded, silent, with the rose in his hand. Long after the travellers have left. And, sometimes, the train.

★ ★ ★

'The newspapers are celebrating your return to the top tier. *Le Miroir des sports* is talking about the phoenix rising . . .'

'. . . from the ashes. I know, Émile, I've heard it a hundred times already.'

Every week, his friend phones him with a complete review of the press, highlighting the laudatory articles, toning the less good ones down a bit. In fact, the sportswriters are insistent: Alfred has regained his muscles and his fighting spirit. Émile is so voluble and enthusiastic that very often, it's Alfred who has to end the call by pretending he has a visitor or a meeting at the club.

However, on this spring day in 1946, the doorbell rings. On the landing is a pallid soldier. He hands Alfred a telex from the Ministry of Armed Forces.

'We regret to confirm that your daughter Annie was gassed two days after her arrival at Auschwitz, on 25 January 1944.'

There's no word of Paule.

11 May
My dear Paule,

Last night I woke up covered in sweat once again. I stayed glued to the window, watching the first glimmers of dawn in a daze. The trees on the other side of the street – plane trees, a few chestnuts and a silver lime – seem to be coming back to life. You would like these trees. They keep going as if nothing had happened. My head is like a vice, exhausting me, driving me mad. Black thoughts rise up, surround me and plunge me into dark waters. Sometimes my fists are clenched so tightly they could break wood.

I feel like a stranger to myself. I must get my head out of the water. Find myself again, calm this rage boiling inside me. The photo of Annie goes everywhere with me. They didn't see her smile. They didn't see her tears when they snatched her soft toy away. And you, our God and protector, what did you see? Come on, tell us! Don't be afraid!

I'm writing to you in my little purple book because I no longer have an address for you. The card I sent to the Boulevard de Sébastopol was returned to me. Yesterday, after training, I walked into town. For no purpose. I walked past the bookshop. In the window, there was a collection of poems with an appealing title, Les Armes miraculeuses

(The Miraculous Weapons).[40] *I went in and leafed through it. The first sentence made me tremble. 'J'attends au bord du monde les-voyageurs-qui-ne-viendront-pas.' (I'm waiting at the edge of the world for travellers who will not come).*

What was the author talking about? He doesn't know us, he can't know. Tell me he's writing a different story. I don't want his words or his book. I ran out of the shop. Tomorrow I'll go back to the station.

The war to end all wars

Why line up for the world championships in Marseille on 8 August 1946, when his heart is nothing more than a cold, dark sun? He knows the risks: a competition too many, useless, grotesque, capable of ruining his record of achievements and making himself ridiculous forever. The very best are there, and they won't have much to fear from him. When it comes to questions from the press, he sticks to providing an update on his health: 'Physically I'm back on top, but my morale is affected.' He should have said 'low'. His brother tells anyone who cares to listen that his eyes have become sad. His brother is right. He doesn't look at them any more. He doesn't switch on the light when he goes into the bathroom. He can't even manage to laugh at a joke, and that's saying something.

He feels this veil over his whole body. He should stop, should protect those who love him from a pathetic spectacle. Nevertheless, he lines up alongside Alex and Yoyo, his two musketeers. Under the watchful eye of Alban the magician; in front of his brothers, his sister and his parents who've come over from Algeria. He lines up like an automaton, guided by a force he doesn't recognize. He can't hear any of the noise from the stands or the announcer's flights of lyricism. He goes into himself, impervious to the world around him. A chrysalis ready to hatch.

Alex is competing in freestyle, Yoyo in breaststroke, Alfred in butterfly. Three times 100 metres, three strokes. To shatter everything. To die for. In his lane, he launches himself into the pool like someone jumping into the void. He bounds through the water, which resists. His arms are burning, tearing apart. He finds his eyes, the real ones that devour the final wall.

He sticks out his tongue.

World record.

For you, my two loves.

Alfred Nakache competing in France, 1946.

Epilogue

Three years after his return from the camps, at the age of thirty-three, Alfred Nakache qualified for the London Olympics – the first games after the war, held in a city that still bore the scars of resistance to Nazism. Five thousand athletes were expected, ten times more than in Berlin in 1936. For Alfred, these games had the taste of a life that was reasserting its rights, even if pain was forever inscribed in his flesh and a new generation of swimmers was dominating the pool, notable among them Alex Jany, his protégé from the Dolphins Club.

On 5 August 1948, at the Empire Pool, Alfred lined up for the quarter finals of the 200 metres breaststroke. His race was a model of power and mastery. Second in his heat; everyone could already picture him with the gold. But Artem took a long time getting out of the water. He felt cramps in his legs, had difficulty recovering, clutched his thigh. He decided that the semi-finals would be his last appearance.

That day, his fears were confirmed. His body let him down. No podium or medal, but a dazzled crowd and the unanimous respect of the press.

These 'games of renewal' were not to smile on France. Alex Jany, the gifted little freestyle swimmer who was expected to reach the top of the podium, missed out, messing up his turns in the 100 and 400 metres freestyle. Alfred immediately flew to his rescue: 'What can you expect, the pools weren't heated last winter, it's impossible to train properly in those conditions.' Fatherly comfort that may not have been terribly convincing, but said everything about the great kindness of Artem. Yoyo saved the day: Georges Vallerey won bronze in the 100 metres backstroke.

Alfred Nakache decided to go overseas. He flew off to the island of Réunion, where he taught sport in schools for several years. He met a woman called Marie, who gave him back his smile and a little faith in the future. On his return to Metropolitan France, he settled down in Sète, on the Mediterranean coast, in a fishermen's house near the corniche. As his niece, Yvette Benayoun-Nakache, would later report, 'There he welcomed all his family to a big party in August, distributing all his medals on impulse in a joyful atmosphere, because he loved life above all else.'

He rarely spoke about the camps. Even less about religion. Every morning at daybreak, he would swim across the Bay of Cerbère, the last small French town before the border with

Spain, covering over a thousand metres in breaststroke or crawl. It became something of a ritual.

On one of these crossings, on 4 August 1983, he was struck down by a heart attack, in the water that had accompanied him throughout his life, between happiness and tragedy. He was sixty-seven years old.

At his last resting place in the Le Py cemetery in Sète, the names of Paule and Annie are engraved alongside his.

★ ★ ★

On 12 March 2021, the French government published profiles of 318 people chosen to represent the history of French diversity. The mayors of French towns and cities were invited to take inspiration from this list when naming streets, avenues, squares and public buildings. Among these women and men was Alfred Nakache. 'He is not only a top-level sportsman,' wrote the members of the commission, 'he is an example of fraternity and commitment.'

Presenting these 'Portraits of France', Emmanuel Macron saluted the heroes of these 'fragmented, fractured stories', who 'contributed to our history but have not yet found their place in our collective memory'.

What became of them?

The deportees of convoy 66

Of the 1,153 deportees of convoy 66, only 45 survived.

Gérard Avran

Gérard Avran was born on 10 April 1927 in Colmar, in the north-east of France. He moved south to Marseille with his family in December 1940. On 10 November 1943, he was arrested with his brother Pierre, his sister Mireille and his mother Rose. His father had already been interrogated. They were all taken to Drancy, then deported to Auschwitz in convoy 66. Rose and Mireille were killed immediately on arrival. In the camp, Gérard made friends with Alfred Nakache. In January 1945, the 'death march' took him to the Mauthausen concentration camp in Upper Austria.

After the liberation, he became a film technician and director for schools. At the age of seventy-three, he decided to bear witness, because 'of the five members of the family, he is the only one who returned from Auschwitz alive'. (www.contreloubli.ch)

Jean Borotra

Tennis champion Jean Borotra, winner of four Grand Slam singles titles and a member of the French Davis Cup team, was a member of the Croix-de-Feu (a nationalist French political movement of the interwar period) and became General Commissioner for Sports in the Vichy government. He was dismissed from this post for having included Alfred Nakache in a tour to North Africa. After being arrested by the Gestapo in 1942, he was detained in Itter Castle, Tyrol, Austria, until May 1945. He was not the subject of any prosecution by the High Court of Justice after the war. He died on 17 July 1994, at the age of ninety-five.

Jacques Cartonnet

Having fled to Sigmaringen in southern Germany, Jacques Cartonnet was sentenced to death in absentia for collaboration by the Toulouse Court of Justice on 19 March 1945. The former swimming champion turned militiaman was eventually arrested in Rome, but made a spectacular escape when, during take-off, he jumped from the military aircraft in which he was to be repatriated to France. He was arrested again by the Italians in November 1947, but after that all trace of him was lost. Alfred Nakache always believed that his rival had denounced him to the Gestapo.

Cheikh Raymond

Born in 1912 in Constantine, Algeria, to a Jewish father and a Catholic mother, Raymond Leyris, also known as Cheikh Raymond, went on to become the undisputed master of Arab-Andalusian music, reaching unparalleled heights of virtuosity and creativity. On 22 June 1961, he was killed by a bullet to the back of the neck in a market in his native city. His murder triggered the departure of Jews from Constantine. His pupil Gaston Ghrenassia, a guitarist in his orchestra, went on to find fame in France as a singer and songwriter under the stage name Enrico Macias.

Willy Holt

On his return to Paris, talented artist Willy Holt, the son of an American father and a French mother, became a production designer and art director for the film industry. He was Oscar-nominated for *Is Paris Burning?* (1966) and won the César for best production design for *Au revoir les enfants* (1987). He died on 22 June 2007, aged eighty-five.

Alex Jany

As Alfred Nakache had predicted, Alex Jany became a great champion. A freestyle specialist, he won twenty-six French championship titles, held fifteen European records and seven world records, and won bronze medals in the 4 x 200 metres freestyle relay at the Olympic Games in 1948 and 1952. He died on 18 July 2001, aged seventy-two.

Noah Klieger

After Auschwitz, Noah Klieger survived the hell of the camp at Dora. His parents, Abraham and Esther, also returned from the camps alive. In 1947, he took part in the struggle for the independence of Israel by joining crew of the *Exodus*. He settled in Tel Aviv and became a renowned sports journalist, a regular correspondent for *L'Équipe* and *France Football* as well as a member of the jury for the Ballon d'Or. He died on 13 December 2018, aged ninety-two.

Léon Lehrer

Born in Paris in 1920 to Jewish parents, refugees from Romania, Léon Lehrer grew up in Montmartre. At the age of twelve, he became an apprentice electrician, while his mother dreamed of his becoming the cantor of a synagogue.

He was arrested in Toulouse on 26 November 1943 along with his sister Louise. Both were transferred to Drancy on 16 December. The following day, Louise was sent on to Auschwitz. In his capacity as an electrician, Léon Lehrer benefitted from semi-freedom in the Drancy camp, before choosing to join his sister via the convoy that left for Auschwitz on 20 January 1944. Now shaved and tattooed, Léon was made part of a *kommando* tasked with lengthening the access ramp at Birkenau. Passing himself off as an electrical engineer, he then joined a *kommando* made up of Frenchmen working in the synthetic rubber factory in the satellite camp of Buna-Monowitz.

He survived the 'death march' of January 1945, which took him to the Buchenwald concentration camp. Transferred in early March to the subcamp at the Sonneberg factory, then evacuated by the SS, he was part of a column that was liberated by the American army in the Bavarian countryside. He was repatriated to Paris by plane from Duisburg. In the face of indifference and lack of understanding from his relatives, he kept silent about his experiences for over fifty years. A few months before his death, in June 2010, at the age of ninety, he said: 'I want to continue to testify in order to make young people understand the barbarity of the Nazis.'

Étienne Mattler

Étienne Mattler, captain of the French national football team, was born in Belfort, in northeastern France, on 24 December 1905. He played for France in the first three World Cups, held in 1930, 1934 and 1938, and won two French championships with FC Sochaux in 1935 and 1938.

In 1942, he joined the resistance and collected weapons dropped by parachute by the Allies. He was arrested by the Gestapo in February 1944 and detained for three months. When tortured, he gave nothing away. His daughter later said that 'to give himself courage and taunt the Germans, he kept a French team tracksuit with him'. He fled to Switzerland in May 1944. Reported as dead by several newspapers in September of that year, he later resurfaced as a sergeant in the forces of Maréchal de Lattre de Tassigny. After a final season at FC Sochaux, in 1946, he opened a bar-tobacconist's in Belfort. He died on 23 March 1986, at the age of eighty.

Alban Minville

As the coach of the Dauphins of Toulouse, much loved by the club's swimmers, Alban Minville was responsible for the success of Christian Talli, Alfred Nakache, Alex Jany, Georges Vallerey and Jean Boiteux. A specialist in butterfly, drawing up the model for its movements, he was innovative with regard to the length of training sessions, the rhythm of the race and strength training outside the pool. A cultural complex in Toulouse was named after him.

Jean Taris

Nicknamed 'the King of the Water', swimmer Jean Taris was the perfect role model for Alfred Nakache, who trained with him in Paris. He broke eight freestyle world records between 1930 and 1932 and was the first French swimmer to go below 60 seconds over 100 metres. Taris was an early proponent of alternate or bilateral breathing: breathing alternately to the right and left every three strokes. In 1932, he won a silver medal in the 400 metres freestyle at the Los Angeles Olympics. He died in Grasse, France, on 10 January 1977, aged sixty-seven.

Georges Vallerey

Georges Vallerey, known as Yoyo, learned to swim in the port of Casablanca, Morocco, under the watchful eye of his father, also named Georges, who was a former champion swimmer. It is also in the port of Casablanca that Yoyo helped rescue more than fifty French sailors on 8 November 1942, the day of the American landings. He was only fifteen years old at the time. Then began his extraordinary career as a champion: he beat the European records for the 100 and 200 metres backstroke in 1945, and the following year, alongside Alfred Nakache, he beat the world record for the 3 x 100 metres medley. A great charmer, he was idolized by the French public. In 1950 he developed nephritis, a kidney condition that made him gain an excessive amount of weight and prevented him from swimming. Despite undergoing a variety of treatments, he died in Casablanca on 4 October 1954, at the age of twenty-six.

Robert Waitz

The son of a doctor of Russian origin and a professor of natural sciences, Robert Élie Waitz was an associate professor at the University of Strasbourg. As a member of the resistance, he was taken to Auschwitz, then to Buchenwald, at the same time as Alfred Nakache. At Buchenwald, he was assigned to block 46, an experimental vaccine research unit where SS doctors used inmates as test subjects, infecting healthy individuals with typhus. After the liberation of the camp, Waitz returned to Strasbourg, where he became a specialist in blood transfusions. At the Nuremberg trials, he testified about the medical experiments undertaken by the Nazis.

In April 1967, on the occasion of the inauguration of the International Monument to the Victims of Fascism at Auschwitz, he said: 'You, the young people of today, never forget what war, totalitarianism, the denial of the human being, the unleashing of racial hatred, sadism and all the basest instincts lead to. Fight these evil forces without respite, because at any moment Neo-Nazism, racism and antisemitism may reappear. Be vigilant, because thousands of war criminals remain unpunished.'

Waitz died of a heart attack on 21 January 1978, aged seventy-seven.

Endnotes

1. Based on the story and testimony of Léon Lehrer.
2. Based on the story and testimony of Gérard Avran.
3. See *Lettres de Drancy*, texts compiled by Antoine Sabbagh
    (Tallandier, 2002). A collection of letters that Louise Jacobsen
    (1924–43) wrote from prison and the Drancy camp was
    published in France in 1989 and also adapted for the stage.
    Gabriel Ramet (1920–95) was later sent to the Mittelbau-Dora
    camp in Thuringia, where he took part in acts of sabotage to
    disrupt the assembly of V-2 rockets at the Mittelwerk factory.
4. Aloïs Brunner is 'the man in the ruling of the "Jewish
    Question" in France', as Annette Wieviorka and Michel
    Laffitte wrote in *'À l'intérieur du camp de Drancy* (Perrin, 2012).
    After his arrival, the French civil servants were driven out of
    the camp, and the police were responsible only for outside
    surveillance. Brunner chose to have the Jewish community
    itself as his sole interlocutor, via the Union générale des
    israélites de France (UGIF, or the Union of French Jews),
    an organization established by the Vichy government at
    Germany's behest. The aim of this strategy was 'in a perverse
    logic that has been trialled since the Nazis came to power
    in Berlin and Vienna, to implicate the Jews in their own
    persecution'.

5. Alfred Nakache told Gérard Avran about his refusal to leave Drancy without his wife and daughter.

6. The convoy transported 1,153 people, including 144 children under the age of fourteen and 81 under the age of nine.

7. The Vélodrome d'Hiver (or Vél d'Hiv) round-up was the largest French deportation of Jews during the Holocaust. It took place in Paris on 16–17 July 1942 at the Winter Velodrome, an indoor cycling track and stadium.

8. Inspired by the memories of Claude S., born in 1933 in Oujda, who lived in Constantine for many years and whose family was close to Paule's.

9. In the words of Claude S.

10. As described in the book by Bertrand Dicale, *Cheikh Raymond, une histoire algérienne* (First, 2011).

11. As described in the biography of Victor Pérez by André Nahum, *Young Perez champion: De Tunis à Auschwitz, son histoire* (Télémaque, 2013).

12. Buster Crabbe, a future Tarzan on screen.

13. Both discriminatory (requiring payment of a poll tax) and protective (granting freedom of worship), *dhimmi* status was applied to non-Muslim subjects, mainly Jews and Christians, of a state under Muslim subgovernment. This right had already been abolished at the time but remained very present in people's minds.

14. In the 1931 census, the population of Constantine included 51,445 Muslims, 36,092 Europeans and 12,058 Jews.

15. Jean Vigo, who died at the age of twenty-nine in 1934, made two cult films, *Zéro de conduite* and *L'Atalante,* which were re-released in France after the war. François Truffaut (1932–84), who saw Vigo's films as a teenager, said he 'owed him his respect'.

16. Jacques Cartonnet, *Nages* (Gallimard, 1935).

17. Germany were the big winners at the Berlin Olympics, with eighty-nine medals, thirty-three of them gold, beating the

USA in the medal tables for the first time (fifty-six medals, twenty-four of them gold). Despite victories in boxing, wrestling and weightlifting, France only finished in sixth place, giving rise to a chorus of criticism in the press. In *L'Auto*, Gaston Meyer and Jacques Goddet were sarcastic: 'Sport in the French style, sport for pleasure. A cavalier, slipshod and risky concept that is no match for the scientific approach and discipline of the Germans.' In *Miroir du monde*, José Germain dealt the death blow: 'In the most secret depths of its stirring heart, France still nourishes a great hope: victory by a miracle.'

18. Jean Taris, *La Joie de l'eau. Ma vie, mes secrets, mon style* (Les Œuvres françaises, 1937).

19. Charles Rigoulot (1903–62), French weightlifter, racing driver and wrestler.

20. Johnny Weissmuller (1904–84), a swimmer with an exceptional record – fifty-two United States championship titles, twenty-eight world records and five Olympic gold medals – was chosen to play Tarzan in 1932 and became the most famous 'Lord of the Jungle' in cinema history.

21. Quoted by Frédéric Mitterrand in *1938, l'œil du cyclone* (XO Éditions, 2022).

22. Louis Gillet, *Rayons et ombres d'Allemagne* (Flammarion, 1937).

23. Presented as a pledge of peace, the Munich agreement, signed on 30 September 1938, came before the evacuation of the Czechs from the Sudetenland and its progressive occupation by German troops.

24. In fact, it was better not to cross his path: Dr Petiot didn't only create fake documents, he was also a serial killer who, after the Liberation, was sentenced to death for twenty-four murders.

25. In the pages of *Au pilori*, Émile Dortignac attributed their success not to their talent but to the ability of the 'chosen people' to unite to make each one of their members succeed. 'Sport serves as a good alibi for circulating ethno-racial

theories forming the basis of antisemitic thought' is the analysis of the historian Doriane Gomet, in 'Rendre les juifs vulnérables par le sport: une stratégie des journaux antisémites', in T. Terret, L. Robène, P. Charroin, S. Héas and Ph. Liotard (eds), *Sport, genre et vulnérabilité au xxe siècle*, Presses universitaires de Rennes, 2013, pp. 317–330.

26. As told in *Plus d'un tour dans ma vie!*, the testimony of Noah Klieger (Elkana, 2014).

27. In his memoirs, *Femmes en deuil sur un camion* (Nil Éditions, 1995), Willy Holt wrote: 'Strictly logically, a person deprived of everything, all hope for the future, will react, without it being thinkable to hold it against him, by plunging alone into the pleasure brought by this unforeseen godsend. Alfred shares his treasure. In this world of distress, savagery, uninterrupted struggle for life, this gesture takes on a dimension of heroism. Other initiatives of the same kind will later confirm the quality of Alfred Nakache, and be an example to me.'

28. The camp de Noé is located south of Toulouse. From February 1941 to the end of summer 1942, 2,500 foreigners were imprisoned there – half of them Jews, the other half Spanish republicans. The nearby camp du Récébédou, in the parish of Portet-sur-Garonne, was the point of departure for convoys to Auschwitz and other extermination camps, via Drancy.

29. *Vous n'aurez pas les enfants* is the title of the remarkable book by Valérie Portheret (XO Éditions, 2020). Of the 108 children who escaped from the camp at Vénissieux, three would be recaptured by the Gestapo, then deported and killed at Auschwitz: Margot Koppel, and Maurice and Gabrielle Teitelbaum.

30. French champion in the 200 metres breaststroke, the 4 x 200 metres freestyle relay, and the 100 metres, 200 metres and 400 metres freestyle.

31. Émile-Georges Drigny, who two years previously had written the profile of Nakache in *Le Miroir des sports*, became president of the French Swimming Federation in 1942. He held the post until 1949.

32. Joseph Pascot was a former fly half of the French rugby team. A colonel in the army, under the Vichy regime, he was the head of Jean Borotra's cabinet, then succeeded him.

33. 'Tracked down by the antisemitic media, in a departure glorified by the sporting press, the swimmer is arrested and deported amid complete media silence', noted the historian Doriane Gomet (*op. cit.*).

34. The Francs-tireurs and partisans-Main-d'œuvre immigrée (FTP-MOI) were units of the Communist resistance which, from April 1942, waged guerrilla warfare against the Nazi occupation in the major cities of France.

35. From Claude S's memories of his own grandmother.

36. According to the testimony of Léon Lehrer.

37. Françoise was the pseudonym of Marie-Louise Dissard. At the head of a resistance network of more than 200 people, she helped, hid and repatriated via Spain more than 700 British and American airmen who had come down on French soil.

38. See the testimony of Robert Guenet in *Georges Vallerey, la vie et la mort d'un grand champion*, by Andrée-Marie Legangneux (Éditions Maroprint, Casablanca, 1954).

39. Six months later, Georges Vallerey and Robert Guenet would receive the Croix de guerre for their heroism.

40. *Les Armes miraculeuses*, by Aimé Césaire, 1946.

Author's note

In 2019, I read a short article about Alfred Nakache's induction into the International Swimming Hall of Fame in Florida. That was how I learned of the existence of this forgotten great French champion, about the tragedy he lived through and also his incredible life force. A 'life against the current', as a newspaper nicely put it. I then immersed myself in the few existing texts about the 'swimmer of Auschwitz', the books by champions who swam with him and the memoirs of deportees who knew him in Auschwitz.

To write this book, I let myself be guided by the ways in which 'Artem' inspired me as I did my background reading. In this 'true novel', the dialogue, some of the situations (his meeting with Paule, in particular) and some secondary characters have been imagined to give the story some body. All the quoted material concerning Alfred Nakache (leaflets, newspaper articles) is authentic, as are the important events in his life that are recounted in these pages:

- his youth in Constantine and his fear of water;
- his rivalry with the antisemitic swimmer Jacques Cartonnet;
- his sporting exploits, the Berlin Games, the attacks in the press, the boycott organized by his friends from the Dauphins after his dismissal from the club, his arrest and deportation to Auschwitz with his wife and daughter;
- the daggger test, Willy Holt's erotic drawings, the secret swims in the company of Noah Klieger, the evidence of Gérard Arvan and Léon Lehrer, the death march, the execution of the boxer Young Perez, the meeting with Roger Foucher-Créteau in Buchenwald and his 'book of memories';
- Nakache's return to Toulouse when all the world thought he was dead, the notification of Annie's death, and the final world record in Marseille, as if thumbing his nose at fate.

I hope this book will contribute in its own way to the duty of remembering and vigilance, now more necessary than ever in the face of antisemitism and all forms of racism.

Bibliography

Abgrall, Fabrice; Thomazeau, François, *1936 – La France à l'épreuve des Jeux olympiques de Berlin*, Alvik Éditions, 2006

Baud, Daniel, *Alfred Nakache, le nageur d'Auschwitz*, Éditions Loubatières, 2009

Bensoussan, Georges; Dietschy, Paul; François, Caroline; Strouk, Hubert (eds), *Sport, corps et sociétés de masse: Le projet d'un homme nouveau*, Armand Colin, coll. 'Recherches', 2012

Brohm, Jean-Marie, *1936 – Jeux olympiques à Berlin*, André Versaille, 2008

Clastres, Patrick (ed.), *Le Sport européen à l'épreuve du nazisme*, exhibition catalogue, Mémorial de la Shoah, Paris, 2011

Dicale, Bertrand, *Cheikh Raymond, une histoire algérienne*, First, 2011

Foucher-Créteau, Roger, *Écrit à Buchenwald:1944–1945*, La Boutique de l'Histoire, 2001

Gomet, Doriane; Bauer, Thomas; Morales, Yves, 'Alfred Nakache, des bassins olympiques au couloir de Drancy: Analyse socio-historique de la carrière d'un champion (1934–1944)', in Laurence Munoz (ed.), *Usages corporels et pratiques aquatiques du xviiie au xxe siècle*, L'Harmattan, 2008

Holt, Willy, *Femmes en deuil sur un camion*, Nil Éditions, 1995

Klieger, Noah, *Plus d'un tour dans ma vie!*, Elkana, 2014

Lehrer, Léon; Zak, Sonia, *Un poulbot à Pitchipoï*, Causette, 1998

Lettres de Drancy, texts compiled and edited by Antoine Sabbagh, Tallandier, 2002; coll. 'Texto', 2019

Mitterrand, Frédéric, *1939, l'œil du cyclone*, XO Éditions, 2022

Nahum, André, *Young Perez champion: De Tunis à Auschwitz, son histoire*, Éditions Télémaque, 2013

Portheret, Valérie, *Vous n'aurez pas les enfants*, XO Éditions, 2020, forewords by Serge Klarsfeld and Boris Cyrulnik; Pocket, 2021

Pourcher, Yves, *Brasse papillon: Le roman d'un collabo*, Gaussen, 2021

Sprawson, Charles, *Héros et nageurs* (original English title: *Haunts of the Black Masseur: The Swimmer as Hero*), Nevicata, 2019

Taris, Jean, *La Joie de l'eau: Ma vie, mes secrets, mon style*, Les Œuvres françaises, 1937

Wieviorka, Annette; Laffitte, Michel, *À l'intérieur du camp de Drancy*, Perrin, 2012

Documentaries

Lashéras, Thierry, *Nage libre*, France 3 Occitanie, 2019

Meunier, Christian, *Alfred Nakache, le nageur d'Auschwitz*, with the voice of Pierre Arditi, 2001

Vigo, Jean, *Taris, le roi de l'eau*, Gaumont, 1931

Acknowledgements

Thank you to my publishers, for their confidence.

To Édith Leblond, who encouraged me to write this novel.

To François-Guillaume Lorrain and Paul Dietschy for their useful advice on reading.

To Damien Naddéo and Pascal Aznar – press attaché and highly skilled swimmer – for the energy deployed with regard to the book.

Thank you to all the team at Archipel.

And lastly, thanks to my nearest and dearest – they will know who they are – for their very precious listening and affection.